COPYRIGHT:

The Complete Guide for Music Educators

D0193367

JAY ALTHOUSE

Published by:

Music in Action

Distributed exclusively by:

Alfred

Alfred Publishing Co., Inc.
P.O. Box 10003
Van Nuys, California 91410-0003

Book design and cover: Meissner Illustration & Design

ISBN 0-939139-07-3

Contents

Preface to the Second Edition

In 1984, when I wrote the first edition of this book, most of us didn't own a VCR and almost none of us had a personal computer. So things have changed, at least technologically. But surprisingly, copyright laws have changed little. The book remained accurate as a useful and practical resource for music educators for nearly a decade and a half. And of course, the principles of copyright haven't changed a bit.

The purpose of this second edition is to bring the book up to date technologically by including chapters on Video and Computers. I've also revised the existing chapters by incorporating any changes in copyright law which have occurred since 1984 and what effect they have on music educators. Perhaps the most notable change is stiffer fines for copyright infringers.

In 1984 I never expected that this book would be received as well as it has been and I am grateful to those of you who purchased the first edition. To those of you who have now purchased the second edition, I hope to help you understand and respect copyright law. Copyright is vital to the creative community and it deserves the respect and support of all music educators. I hope that both you and your music department respect copyright, perhaps with a department copyright policy. And most importantly, set an example and teach your students to respect it, too.

Jay Althouse

PART I
Introduction

 # *Why This Book?*

I understand your problems. You're an elementary music teacher and you've just found a wonderful musical play for your fifth graders to perform at the P.T.A. Christmas program. But it would cost a bundle to purchase parts for all your students and your principal refuses to give you any money. It would be such a great learning experience, though, so you buy a director's score and one student part which you photocopy for your students.

You're a senior high band director and the only published band arrangement of a pop song your band wants to perform is terrible. "I can arrange it better than that," you say, so you arrange it yourself.

You're a college brass instructor and your senior trumpet major wants to perform a solo from your personal library at his senior recital. The solo is published by an obscure French publisher and it cost $15 back in 1975, so Lord knows what it costs now! If you order it today, it probably won't arrive until after your student graduates, and besides, it's probably out of print. So you make a photocopy for your student and tell him to keep it with your compliments.

I understand your problems.

But I also understand the problems of the music publisher who spent thousands of dollars producing that wonderful Christmas musical only to see an order for one director's score and one student part. If the publisher sees too many orders like that he might think twice about publishing another musical next year.

And I understand the problems of the writer who worked

months on that Christmas musical, making sure every line and staging direction was just right. She wonders, after she gets her first royalty statement, why her publisher sold 1000 scores but only 2200 student parts when, in fact, the ratio of scores to student parts, based on the number of speaking and singing roles, should be more like six or seven student parts to each score.

I understand their problems, too.

This is not a how-to book—how to copyright your original songs. Nor is a book of do's and don'ts. Do's and don'ts are for little posters hanging above photocopying machines in public libraries. This is a book of why's and why not's: why, under certain circumstances you *may* photocopy music, and why under other circumstances you may not; why you need permission to arrange a pop song; why you cannot be denied permission to record a song but why you must pay a royalty on each copy distributed. I'll list the legal why's and why not's. And I'll describe the moral why's and why not's too.

I believe music educators are genuinely interested in copyright. Most of us have a general understanding of copyright but we'd like to know more. And I think we're a little bit scared or it. "What if I do something wrong? Can I be fined, or sent to jail? Does the Copyright Office have agents who check on schools?" I hope to dispel a lot of myths with this book. For starters, no the FBI does not have agents snooping on music teachers. There may be some other snoops you have to look out for, though, and I'll discuss that in later chapters.

Preparing to write a book, I've found, is no different than preparing to compose a musical work. First, you organize, and you establish a form. I've organized this book into four sections which loosely resemble the classic sonata form. So that's how I've identified the sections. You're reading Part I, the Introduction, now. Part II, the Exposition, covers the history of copyright and an overview of the present United States copyright law, the Copyright Act of 1976. Part III, the Development, relates the Copyright Act of 1976 to specific aspects of music education, such as photocopying, recording, performing and arranging. Part IV, the Recapitulation, contains a glossary, addresses, and specific information which you may want to refer to later.

I urge you to read Parts I and II of this book before you begin any chapter in Part III. The specific information presented in Chapters 5 through 11 is based on an understanding of Chapters 2 through 4. So if you're planning to make a recording, don't jump straight to Chapter 7. Read Part II first.

Copyright didn't fall from the sky in 1976 with the current United States Copyright Act. It developed gradually over the last 300 years. I want you to understand that development and I want you to understand exactly what copyright is. It's not that difficult or complex. Really!

This book developed out of a thorough analysis of the Copyright Act of 1976 as it pertains to music, a study of the history of copyright, my experience handling copyrights for an educational music publisher throughout the 1980's, and my experience as a composer, arranger, and musician. I have not attempted to cover every conceivable copyright issue in this book. But I have tried to answer the questions most frequently asked about copyright by music educators.

I am not an attorney and this book should not be considered as legal advice. If you have specific questions about the legality of matters pertaining to copyright, you should consult an attorney—preferably one specializing in copyright law.

Nor do I represent to speak for music publishers as a group. Publishers and copyright owners have different views and opinions on how to handle the many requests for the use of their works. Some are very liberal in permitting use of their works; others prefer to restrict the use of their works. So for specific information on the use of a specific copyrighted musical work, you should always contact the copyright owner of the work.

Finally, this book pertains to copyright laws in the United States only.

PART II
Exposition

2 *What is Copyright?*

Copyright is, literally, the right to copy. And the main purpose of copyright in the United States is to produce a public benefit. Period.

That's what copyright is and why it exists. Copyright is a body of laws designed "to promote the progress of science and the useful arts, by securing for limited times to authors...the exclusive right to their respective writings." That comes straight from the United States Constitution.

Surprised? You say you thought the purpose of copyright was to enrich publishers, or to limit your access to music? Wrong. On both counts. In fact, copyright laws foster creativity and the distribution of artistic works. Indeed, the arts flourish in countries with strong copyright laws.

Copyright is a Right

Note that copyright is a right derived from authority granted to Congress by our Constitution. Our founding fathers were big on rights. They granted to creative citizens the exclusive right to their creations. Inventors could obtain patents and writers copyrights. Without that right a writer or composer has no protection against the unlimited free use of his work by others. If everyone has free access to a writer's work, it has no material value. No potential income. The only incentive to create, then, is personal satisfaction.

Now, personal satisfaction is great, but it doesn't put food on the table. Nor does it enable a writer or his publisher to invest in the publication of his writings. Copyright alone creates the financial incentive to publish. And without publication there would be little dissemination of creative works to the public.

Think about it. You may have heard publishers say that photocopying might drive them out of business. There's some truth to that. If copyright laws were repealed tomorrow and photocopies were legalized there would be no financial incentive to publish. With no one required to pay for their product, publishers would cease publication. How long do you think Exxon would stay in business if everyone could pump gasoline for free?

We, the public, are the main beneficiaries of copyright laws. And we have a moral and legal obligation to abide by those laws. If everyone ignored copyright laws, the effect would be the same as no copyright laws at all. Copyright makes publication—and the public dissemination of knowledge possible.

Which brings us to a secondary purpose for copyright: rewarding the creators for their writings. In music, here's how it usually works:

Let's say I write a piece of choral music. I think it's good but it's just sitting on my desk. I haven't the time, the inclination, nor the resources to engrave, print, promote, and distribute my composition. I need someone to provide those services for me. I need a publisher. A publisher, in turn, needs a product—a musical composition. We each have something the other needs and, as a composer, here's where my rights under copyright laws begin to translate into money. Under rights granted by our Constitution, I "own" my composition—or more accurately, I own the exclusive right to my composition. It follows that if I own something, I can sell it, and that is exactly what I do. I "sell" (or actually assign) my product, my exclusive right to my composition, to a publisher. In most cases, the publisher "pays" me with a royalty on each copy sold.

If the piece is a success, we both make some money. That's how the system works and copyright makes it all possible.

Copyright is an Intangible

Another important point about copyright: it is an intangible. It is not a physical property such as a personal computer or an automobile. Further, ownership of copyright in a creative work is separate and distinct from ownership of a physical copy of the work. An artist, for example, may sell an original painting but still own the copyright in the painting. The purchaser owns the physical copy but the artist retains his copyright. This may be valuable to the painter if he wants to make and sell prints of the painting, for example. Similarly, when you purchase a published musical composition, you own a *copy* of the composition and not the composition itself. That's all.

To illustrate the intangible aspect of copyright, I like to use the following analogy.

Let's say I own one share of General Motors stock valued at $50. I "own" a part of General Motors—a minute part, to be sure. But what do I *really* own? Well, I have a stock certificate but that's just a piece of paper which certainly isn't worth $50. And I can't cash in my share for $50 worth of nuts and bolts or a tire.

I own an intangible—a share in a corporation. The value of my share of GM stock is determined by the public demand for GM stock. If the company earns a profit and the demand for the stock increases, the value of my share increases. If the company goes broke, my stock has no value. So it is with a song. If it's a good one and the demand for it is great, the value of the copyright is great. If the song's a loser and no one wants to buy it, the copyright has no value. Copyrights, like stocks, can be winners and losers.

Let's carry my stock analogy one step further. Suppose you buy a new Chevrolet from a General Motors dealer for $20,000. Even though you've paid General Motors far more for your car than I have for my single share of stock, you are *not* a part owner of GM, as I am. You simply own one of GM's products. Again it's the same with music. When you buy a piece of published music you own a product—a copy—issued by the copyright owner. You do not own the music itself.

Only General Motors can manufacture Chevrolets and only a copyright owner can print copies of his music. GM doesn't have a problem with people making copies of its cars, though; there are no drive-thru Xerox machines—yet! But copyright owners do have a problem. Each year music educators make thousands of unauthorized photocopies of copyrighted musical works.

Perhaps we think we're saving money by photocopying, or we're doing it in the name of education, or we think just one copy won't do any harm. The harm is not that a publisher may earn less money, or that a composer may have to supplement his income by selling Chevrolets. The real harm is that the public benefit of copyright—the tens of thousands of published musical works now available for sale—may disappear.

 **3** *History of Copyright*

The history of copyright is the history of communications. Ever since the invention of the printing press, man has strived to copy almost everything he has written. In the United States, our present copyright law, the Copyright Act of 1976, is the result of over 500 years of technological advances in the art of making copies and nearly 300 years of copyright legislation in the English-speaking world. For three centuries legislators both in the United States and around the world have grappled with the problem of how to balance the public's need for information with the author's right to his writings. The Act of 1976 didn't solve that problem but it came closer than any copyright statute ever written.

Early Copyright Laws

Before Johann Gutenberg invented movable type in the fifteenth century, there was no need for copyright protection. The only way to copy anything was by hand. An author had little fear that anyone would take the time and effort to hand copy the book *he* had meticulously copied by hand. The public, on the other hand, had little access to scholarly writings. But the printing press and Gutenberg's movable type changed all that.

Suddenly any man with a printing press could copy anything ever written. And he usually did. Books. Pamphlets. Articles. Maps. Printers printed them all in vast quantities and without permission from or payment to anyone.

In 1556, the King of England decided things had gotten out of hand. Actually what bothered him was not that printers were ripping off authors, but that some printers were publishing articles and pamphlets critical of him. So Parliament enacted the Licensing Act which licensed publishers and created the Stationer's Company, a kind of censor for the king. It also prohibited the printing of any book unless it was registered by a licensed publisher with the Stationer's Company. It worked. The number of pamphlets critical of the king dropped dramatically.

The Licensing Act had a secondary effect on the publishing industry, however. When a publisher registered a book with the Stationer's Company, all other publishers were prohibited from publishing it. In effect, a publisher who registered a book obtained a monopoly on its publication. Thus began the practice of governments granting exclusive publishing rights.

It is important to note that the Licensing Act was *not* a copyright act. Its purpose was censorship and not the protection of authors' rights.

In 1694 the Licensing Act expired and the unauthorized printing and pirating of all types of publications began anew. Reputable publishers, who had become accustomed to the financial benefits they enjoyed under the Licensing Act, petitioned Parliament for relief. Parliament responded in 1709 with the Statute of Anne which is recognized as the first true copyright act anywhere in the world. Its purpose was indeed the protection of the rights of authors. Under the Statute of Anne, authors were granted copyright protection for their works for a period of 14 years, with a renewal term of an additional 14 years.

The First American Copyright Acts

Most of the American colonies enacted copyright statutes during the eighteenth century and in 1789, when the new nation got around to writing a constitution and Congress began enacting its first laws, copyright was given a top priority. The first federal copyright statute, enacted in 1790, afforded copyright protection to the authors of books, maps, and charts. (Map making was important to a new nation comprised largely of wilderness.) Like the Statute of Anne, the Act of 1790 granted copyright protection for 14 years with a 14 year renewal term.

During the nineteenth century Congress enacted a series of copyright statutes, each one broadening the scope of copyright protection to new and different artistic and creative works. In 1831, in a general revision of the 1790 Act, copyright protection was first provided to composers of musical works. Photographs received protection in 1865 (Remember Matthew Brady and his Civil War photographs?), and works of fine art and dramatic works in 1870.

By the turn of the twentieth century, technology was moving faster than copyright. New technologies, such as player pianos (one of the first inventions by which a non-musician could actually hear music performed by a machine) wreaked havoc with court interpretations of copyright laws which were largely based on Britain's 1709 Statute of Anne. In 1905 President Theodore Roosevelt called for a new copyright act and four years later Congress delivered the Copyright Act of 1909.

The Copyright Act of 1909

The Act of 1909 significantly changed U.S. copyright law. First of all, it increased the term of copyright protection from 14 years with a 14 year renewal term to 28 years with a 28 year renewal term. In the area of music the Act of 1909 addressed the issue of player pianos and piano rolls. In the early years of this century, player pianos were extremely popular and with the Act of 1909 Congress recognized copyright owners' right to reproduce their songs on piano rolls—or "mechanical instruments" as they were called, since Congress wanted to include any other mechanical means of reproducing music. Hence, the right to record musical works became known as the "mechanical right," and it still called that today.

However, Congress also feared that the largest and richest piano roll companies would monopolize the industry by paying large sums of money for the exclusive mechanical rights to the most popular songs. Congress solved this problem by creating the "compulsory mechanical license." Under terms of the compulsory mechanical license, once a copyright owner had granted permission for the first recording of his song, *anyone* could record the song provided he paid the copyright owner a fee of 2¢ for each recording manufactured. In other words, the copyright owner could control the *first* recording of his song but thereafter he lost the right to control recordings of the song. The compulsory mechanical license was the most controversial and unique aspect of the Act of 1909. In retrospect, it was a bold move, and it served the musical community—both users and creators—well for decades.

The Act of 1909 also confirmed an element of copyright which had been recognized only a few decades earlier: the right of performance. The right to perform dramatic works prevented unauthorized performances of plays and operettas, a practice which was prevalent in the United States well into the nineteenth century. Performance rights in musical works had been recognized in 1897. The Act of 1909 reaffirmed the performance right but placed a limitation on it: only "public" performances made "for profit" could be subject to control by copyright owners.

The Copyright Act of 1909 remained in effect until 1978.

4 Copyright Today: The Copyright Act of 1976

Although the Copyright Act of 1909 brought United States copyright law into the twentieth century, it was unable to keep pace with advances in communications technology. By the 1970's there were dozens of new communications devices such as radio, television, records, cassettes, 8-track tapes, photocopying machines, communications satellites, and computers. And the piano roll had become almost obsolete. Actually, the Act of 1909 coped with technological advances fairly well, considering that in 1909 the printing press was the main disseminator of information. But throughout the twentieth century courts struggled to apply the Act of 1909 to questions which Congress could not have imagined in 1909.

By 1955 it was obvious that the United States needed a new copyright statute and Congress authorized the Register of Copyrights to study and research the entire issue of copyright. Thus began twenty-one years of studies, recommendations, hearings, reports, and proposals, which finally resulted in the passage by the 94th Congress of the Copyright Act of 1976. It became law on January 1, 1978.

In one of his reports to Congress, the Register of Copyrights (By the way, that's the correct title: the *Register* of Copyrights, not the Registrar.) wrote that "the basic legislative problem is to insure that the copyright law provides the necessary monetary incentive to write, produce, publish, and disseminate creative works, while at the same time guarding against the danger that these works will not be disseminated and used as fully as they should because of copyright restrictions."

Once again Congress had to balance the rights of authors and writers with the public's need for information. Because the so-called copyright industries—the communications industries such as television, motion pictures, radio, record companies, and publishers—had become so huge, the problem was more complicated than ever. The balance needed to be perfect, or as close to perfect as possible.

Duration of Copyright

The Act of 1976 and a subsequent Copyright Term Extension Act passed in 1998 provide for the following terms of copyright.

Works published between 1923 and 1963 have an initial 28 year term and must be renewed for an additional 67 year term for a total of 95 years. You should assume that any work which achieved any success or popularity has been renewed.

Works published between 1964 and 1977 have an initial 28 year term plus an automatic 67 year second term for a total of 95 years.

Works published after 1977 have a term of the life of the author plus 70 years, or in the case of works with multiple authors, 70 years after the death of the last surviving author. This brings the U.S. in line with most European countries which have copyright terms of life plus 70 years.

Works published before 1923 are in the Public Domain.

Divisibility of Copyright

Before the Act of 1976, copyright was generally considered a single right—basically the right to copy. But because technology had created so many new ways to "copy" a work, the Act of 1976 considers copyright to be a group of rights lumped together under the term "copyright." Further, it considers each of those rights to be independent of the others. In other words, a copyright owner can deal with each of his rights separately. Thus, we hear of novelists talking of "movie rights," "stage rights," "publishing rights," "television rights," "foreign rights," and so on. Courts had previously recognized the divisibility of copyright, but the Act of 1976 was the first U.S. statute to recognize this aspect of copyright.

So when you think of copyright, remember that it is not one single right but a group of rights. And, to use a common analogy, think of a copyright owner as a man holding a group of sticks banded together. He can rent or sell any of his sticks. And he can rent or sell them separately or all together.

It is important, also, to recognize that copyright begins with the author. He is the first to hold all the sticks. In the field of music, as I described in Chapter 2, a composer usually turns over all his rights—all his sticks—to a music publisher in return for a royalty. The publisher, then, becomes the owner of all rights in the composition. So be advised that the copyright owner of a piece of published music is usually, but not always, the publisher of the printed edition.

Exclusive Rights of Copyright Owners

The Copyright Act of 1976 grants to copyright owners five exclusive rights. That's all—just five rights. And only four of those rights really pertain to music.

But those are five broad, sweeping rights and the law immediately places many limitations, known as "Fair Uses," on them. If there were no limitations on these exclusive rights the balance between copyright owners and the public would be too much in favor of copyright owners. The limitations restore the balance.

I'll describe the five exclusive rights in the rest of this chapter and, because the limitations are so important, I'll describe them in detail in Part III of this book.

(1) The right to reproduce the copyrighted work in copies or phonorecords.

The right to reproduce a work is still the most fundamental right afforded a copyright owner. Without this right, the public would have unlimited, free access to copyrighted works. This right is the basis for publication and recording of musical works. The right to "copy" a work is not limited to printed copies. Rather, it extends to copies in any form. The term "phonorecords" pertains to the many ways in which a work can be recorded aurally including CD's, cassettes, vinyl records, midi disks, and so on. Some copyrighted works like plays and shows, for example can be recorded visually, too. For music educators, there are several important limitations on this right and I'll discuss them in Chapters 5 and 6.

(2) The right to perform the copyrighted work publicly.

You may be surprised to learn that the copyright owner, alone, is granted the right to perform his copyrighted work in public. Unlike the performance right granted in the Act of 1909, the performance right under the 1976 Act is not limited to public performances "for profit." But don't worry—your Spring band or choral concert probably doesn't violate this right. There are a whole host of limitations placed on it and those limitations cover most of the performances made by your performing groups. There are exceptions, though, and I'll get to them in Chapter 8.

(3) The right to prepare derivative works based on the copyrighted work.

In music, this means that the copyright owner has the exclusive right to make arrangements of his copyrighted musical work. Obviously, this is an important right for music publishers—and especially for music publishers who specialize in providing printed music for music educators. Translations, transcriptions, and other adaptations are derivative works, too. I'll discuss this right further in Chapter 9.

(4) The right of public distribution of a copyrighted work.

This right is closely linked to the right to make copies. It too is a valuable right for music publishers who print music for music educators. But it is more important to recording companies who, under this right, can prevent the sale of pirated or counterfeit recordings. Chapter 7 covers this right extensively.

(5) The right to display a copyrighted work publicly.

For composers, this right has limited applicability. For visual artists such as painters, sculptors, or film makers it is very important. It gives them control over the showing and exhibition of their works. More in Chapter 10.

PART III
Development

 **5** *Photocopying: Music*

Photocopying is one of the biggest problems facing the educational music publishing industry today. And music educators, I think, are aware of it. In fact, you may have purchased this book to find out what you may or may not photocopy. Unauthorized photocopying is a flagrant violation of copyright laws that, unlike budget cuts, could be eliminated if music educators adhered to the law. That's what upsets music publishers. Every unauthorized copy is a lost sale and lower sales mean less income for publishers which, in turn, means less income in the form of lower royalties for composers.

During the 1970's educational music publishers and organizations such as the Music Publishers' Association, the Church Music Publishers' Association, and the National Music Publishers' Association felt music educators needed to be educated on the matter of copyright. Educators, they believed, were unaware of the legal and moral implications of photocopying. With the passage of the Copyright Act of 1976, they undertook the responsibility of educating music educators with pamphlets, booklets, articles in journals, and speakers at conventions.

This educational program had mixed results. Music educators were indeed educated but photocopying didn't go away. Today, more than 20 years after the 1976 Act became law, most of us realize that unauthorized photocopying is both legally and morally wrong, yet many of us continue to do it. Why?

Justifications for Photocopying

Some of us have justified photocopying with many reasons, some of which are totally false.

My budget has been cut again and photocopies are the only way I can afford new music. Suppose your band needed a new tuba and you didn't have the funds. Would you steal it? Anyone who relies on this argument is not on solid ground—legally or otherwise.

Music is too expensive. Everything is more expensive than it used to be but I've researched all manner of printed and published products and I can say without hesitation that music has increased less in price over the years than most printed products.

As an example, in the late 1960's, when I was in high school, choral octavos cost 30¢. Today (1998) they're about $1.25 to $1.50, approximately five times what they cost then. During my senior year in high school, my English composition teacher required each of her students to purchase a paperback thesaurus. Mine cost 60¢; I know because I still use it and it is lying, dog-eared and worn, next to my computer as I write this. Today, a similar thesaurus in my local bookstore costs $5.95, ten times the 1960's price.

That's just one example but there are dozens of others. I can remember when greeting cards cost about the same as a choral octavo, too. Try and find a greeting card today for $1.50.

An argument often heard in conjunction with this one is that photocopying is cheaper than buying published music. When I wrote the first edition of this book in 1984 I could say this was rarely true but I must admit that it is more true today. But that's not because the price of music has gone up so much since 1984. Rather, it's because the price of photocopying has come down. Still, the biggest flaw in this argument is: shoplifting is cheaper than buying, but few of us do it.

Having admitted that photocopying may be cheaper than buying published copies, I can hear a few readers asking, "Well, why then does an eight page choral octavo cost $1.40 if I can copy each of the eight pages at 6¢ a copy at my local copy shop?"

Music is more than black symbols printed on white paper. If the printer was the only person who had to be compensated for the music, yes, I guess an eight page choral octavo could sell for 50¢, if you were willing to seek out the printer who published it. But there are many other creative people involved in the creation of a piece of music, the most important of whom is the composer, who deserves to be compensated every time a copy of his music is sold. To say that a piece of choral music is worth only 50¢—the cost of the printing alone—is to deny that the music has any value other than that of the paper, ink, and the printer's time. As creative people we should value music more than that.

How about this argument? *One copy won't hurt.* To this argument a federal judge overseeing a copyright infringement suit once replied, "Babies are still being born one at a time but the world is rapidly becoming overpopulated." (Guess which side he ruled for in that trial.) Single photocopies add up and the result, nationwide, is a huge amount of lost income for publishers and composers. Music education is rapidly becoming overpopulated with photocopies.

I need it now. Sometimes the immediate need for a copy is a legitimate reason for making a photocopy. Sometimes it isn't. I'll discuss this in greater detail later in this chapter.

My principal told me to photocopy (or "The Devil made me do it!" excuse.) The fact that an infringement was ordered by a higher authority does not eliminate liability. It's still an infringement and both of you are infringers.

Everyone does it. Well, most everyone drives a few miles

per hour over the speed limit on the interstates, too. But if you're caught doing 68 in a 65 m.p.h. zone you've broken the law and, if the trooper can make it stick, you're going to have to pay the fine, aren't you? Problem is, the fines for copyright infringement are a lot higher than a speeding ticket.

They're for "educational use." That's true. But suppose your principal asked you to work without pay because your services were for "educational use." The fact is, schools have to pay for almost all the products and services they use from textbooks and electricity to bus drivers' salaries. Educational use in no way means free use.

There are other reasons to justify photocopying but I really believe most music educators have a general idea that photocopying is both legally and morally wrong. My theory is that most people don't want to break copyright laws but, doggone it, it's so much simpler to copy music than to buy it.

Photocopy machines have made us lazy, impatient, selfish, and a little bit spoiled. We have an enormous appetite for information and we want it satisfied quickly. A nearby photocopier can satisfy that appetite. Instead of waiting weeks for purchase orders, deliveries, and back orders, we have in our hands exactly what we wanted in a matter of seconds. Neat. Clean. Cheap. Fast. With plenty of handy rationalizations to justify what we did. Besides, no one's checking up on us, and even if they did, no court would find a music teacher guilty of a criminal offense for making a photocopy, right?

Courts have and more courts will in the future.

The 1970's and 1980's were a period of high-profile copyright cases involving music publishers and educational institutions as well as churches. The most visible cases involved Longwood College in Virginia, the Texas system of higher education, and the Archdiocese of Chicago. In the latter case, Federal courts initially ordered the Diocese to pay over $3 million to a music publisher specializing in music for the Catholic liturgy though the amount was eventually reduced and the Diocese paid $190,000.

The 1990's have been relatively quiet with few music copyright suits involving educators. Indeed, I've had many teachers who feel strongly about copyright ask me why publishers haven't pursued educational infringers more frequently in the courts. The answer is that, as publishers who depend upon the business of educators for a livelihood, we're somewhat reluctant to do so. We certainly don't think of our customers as our adversaries.

And yet, it will happen again. My best guess is that the next lawsuit involving music copyright infringement in the schools will be brought against a school by a publisher who feels he has nothing to lose. That's what the publisher who brought suit against the Archdiocese of Chicago felt.

How might a publisher become aware of an infringing teacher or school? In many ways. Believe me, a publisher doesn't have to leave his office to hear about photocopying. I spent nearly eight years in the copyright department of an educational publisher and the letters we received telling us of photocopying by music educators always amazed me. We received letters from parents who knew it was wrong, from church members, from teachers whose principals instructed them to photocopy. You never know who might observe your unauthorized photocopies and try to turn you in.

The most interesting letter I ever received on the subject of photocopying came from a defeated and disgruntled school board candidate who apparently felt the urge to get even with the school system by blowing the whistle on all illegal photocopying by the music department.

And how did I respond to these letters? Well, not by first instituting a lawsuit. If the letter named the teacher involved— and they usually did—I would draft a letter to the principal of the school saying something like:

> It has been brought to our attention that Mr.—, the choral director in your school, has been making unauthorized and illegal copies of music published by us.
>
> Is this true? If so, would you please confirm that all such photocopies have been destroyed and that you agree not to make such copies in the future. We trust you understand that making unauthorized photocopies is a copyright infringement under federal copyright law.

That letter always generated a quick response and the response was always the same: the infringing copies were destroyed and another principal and music educator were educated (albeit in a less than positive manner) on the consequences of copying. I can only guess what the conversation would have been between the principal and the music teacher. How would your principal handle it with you?

I would rather you stop photocopying for moral rather than legal reasons. Better you support the creation of new works by buying them than by worrying about the threat of a lawsuit. Nevertheless, the legal consequences must not be overlooked. Under current copyright law, the copyright owner of a musical work has the exclusive right to "reproduce the copyrighted work in copies." Clearly, most photocopies of a musical work are made without the consent of the copyright owner and are infringements of this right.

In a criminal case a federal court can, by law, fine infringers from $500 to $20,000 per infringement, although it can go as low as $200 per work infringed if it feels the infringer was truly unwary of the law. On the other hand, a court can go as high as $100,000 in cases involving intentional and willful infringement, though such fines are usually reserved for manufacturers of pirated CD's or cassettes. Most copyright cases are civil suits, however, and in those cases the copyright owner can sue for damages.

Fair Uses

As discussed in Chapter 3, the purpose of copyright laws is the dissemination to the public of creative works. Congress recognized this by placing limitations on the exclusive rights granted to copyright owners. These limitations are known as Fair Uses.

The doctrine of Fair Use has been recognized for decades by the courts but the Act of 1976 was the first U.S. copyright act to give statutory recognition to Fair Use. In general, Fair Use is subject to interpretation by the courts, but Section 107 of the 1976 Act describes the factors a court should consider in determining Fair Use. These factors are:

1. the purpose and character of the use, including whether such use is of a commercial nature or is for non-profit educational purposes;

2. the nature of the copyrighted work;

3. the amount and substantiality of the portion used in relation to the copyrighted work as a whole; and

4. the effect of the use upon the potential market for or value of the copyrighted work.

In other words... Who copied it, how, and why, what kind of a work is it, how much was copied, and what effect does the copying have on the market value of the work?

These are the factors which a court shall "consider" in determining Fair Use. They must be considered together and not individually. The argument that a copy was made "for educational use" will not be necessarily be upheld by factor #1 if it violates factor #4. Note also that a lack of financial gain of the infringer is not a factor. Under certain circumstances, however, photocopying a musical work can be a Fair Use. What are those circumstances?

Fair Use Guidelines for Photocopying Music

Throughout the years leading to the passage of the Copyright Act of 1976, representatives of various groups of copyright owners and copyright users met with Congress in attempts to hammer out guidelines for Fair Uses. Book publishers met with librarians, recording companies met with juke box operators, and so on. In the case of printed music, representatives of the Music Publishers' Association (mainly publishers of serious and educational music) and the National Music Publishers' Association (primarily pop music publishers) met with representatives of the Music Educators' National Conference, the National Association of Schools of Music and the Music Teachers National Association. The publisher organizations represented copyright owners and the music educators' organizations represented copyright users— the two groups whose interests Congress intended to serve. These organizations developed a set of guidelines which would be considered Fair Uses of copyrighted music. Two of those guidelines pertain specifically to photocopying. The guidelines also list specific prohibitions on certain types of photocopying.

Please realize that these guidelines are not laws. They are simply guidelines which a court shall consider in determining Fair Use. Those Fair Uses are:

(1) Emergency copying to replace purchased copies which for any reason are not available for an imminent performance, provided purchased replacement copies shall be substituted in due course.

Simple. Obvious. A Fair Use.

One of your sopranos is participating in a district choral festival next week but the required music hasn't arrived yet. You make photocopies from your personal library. It's a Fair Use—provided you don't cancel your order.

Another example: your eighth grade clarinet player has misplaced the solo he hoped to perform in the spring concert. You make a photocopy from another student's copy and order a new copy for the first student. Another Fair Use. Remember, you must order a replacement copy.

To a certain extent, this Fair Use justifies the "I need it now" argument. Emergency copies are permissible, but only if you order purchased copies to replace them.

(2) For academic purposes other than performance, single or multiple copies of excerpts of works may be made, provided that the excerpts do not comprise a part of the whole which would constitute a performable unit such as a section, movement, or aria, but in no case more than 10 percent of the whole work. The number of copies shall not exceed one copy per pupil.

Please, *please* note that this Fair Use is for purposes *other than performance*. The intent here is to allow copies of brief sections of works for study. A theory teacher may, for example, copy an excerpt from a work—say, an interesting modulation or an unusual harmonization—and distribute the copies to his class for analysis. This Fair Use is pretty much limited to the music classroom.

Under the Fair Use guidelines, the following are expressly prohibited:

(1) Copying to create or replace or substitute for anthologies, compilations or collective works.

Making your own songbooks for your elementary students just won't do. Neither will creating an anthology of study pieces for your private piano students.

(2) Copying of or from works intended to be "consumable" in the course of study or teaching such as workbooks, exercises, standardized tests and answer sheets and like material.

Self-explanatory. Printed music, like workbooks, exercises, and standardized tests, is a consumable product, too. It is not permissible to order thirty copies of a choral octavo, file those copies away and make thirty copies to distribute to your choir, replacing lost and damaged photocopies with more photocopies in order to save the cost of replacing those lost copies.

(3) Copying for the purpose of performance except for emergency copying to replace purchased copies as outlined in (1) of the Fair Uses.

Let me repeat that: copying for the purpose of performance—any performance—is expressly prohibited. The only exception is the Fair Use of emergency photocopies to replace purchased copies. Basically, if you plan to perform it, don't copy it. And I don't mean just performing a work in concert. Rehearsing a work, under the law, is a performance.

(4) Copying for the purpose of substituting for the purchase of music, except as in Fair Uses (1) and (2).

This prohibition neatly summarizes the entire agreement reached between the groups of music publishers and educators. If a photocopy results in a lost sale it will not be considered a Fair Use. If a publisher sells it and you want it, don't copy it. Buy it.

(5) Copying without inclusion of the copyright notice which appears on the printed copy.

If you make a legitimate Fair Use photocopy under one of the guidelines, you must include the copyright notice which usually appears at the bottom of the first page of music.

Out-of-Print Music and Other Dilemmas

Under prohibition (4) above, I said that if a publisher sells a piece of music and you want it, buy it. What if the publisher no longer sells it? What if it's out of print, or available only as a part of a collection? The answer: ask for permission to copy.

Out-of-print works. There is no Fair Use which permits you to photocopy a work simply because it's out of print.

Copyright protection is not related in any way to the print status of a piece of music.

As outlined in Chapter 4, works published prior to 1978 remain protected by copyright for 75 years. For works copyrighted after January 1, 1978, copyright subsists until 50 years after the death of the writer. So an out-of-print work published and copyrighted in 1950 is still protected by copyright—and will be until 2025. All the rights granted to the copyright owner remain in force, even though the work is out of print. Photocopying an out-of-print work is no less an infringement than copying one that's in print.

What to do, then? Write the copyright owner of the piece and ask for permission to make copies. Some publishers now provide information on how to obtain permission to make copies of out-of-print works on their websites. Advise how many copies you wish to make and for what purpose. The copyright owner may grant you permission to make the copies at no charge or he may charge a fee, usually based on the number of copies you wish to make and, perhaps, the length of the work. Why charge a fee even though the work is out of print?

Generally, publishers feel that composers should be compensated for the use of their works and money collected by publishers from copying fees is usually shared with the composer. One of a publisher's duties is to exploit its works as fully as possible. Many publishers feel they would be neglecting their obligations to their composers by granting free permission to make photocopies. Others simply feel it is important to stress that music has a value. After all, music is the only product a music publisher has to sell. As a Nashville songwriter once said: "A lot of people think that music comes from the radio like milk comes from the supermarket, leaving both the songwriter and the cow high and dry."

There is always the possibility that a publisher may deny your request to make photocopies of an out-of-print work or that he may never reply. Why? I don't know.

A publisher is under no obligation to grant you such permission but, to me, it just doesn't make sense to say no. The only legitimate reasons I can think of are that the publisher no longer owns the copyright (in which case he should tell you who does) or that he is prevented from doing so under the terms of his contract with the composer. I will not, however, defend a publisher who doesn't respond to your request or who takes more than a month to reply. Publishers, I believe, have a responsibility to respond promptly to such request.

If you get a negative reply, or no reply, you don't have the permission, so don't make the copies.

Photocopying works from collections. Suppose you want one work contained in a published collection or folio but you don't want to buy the entire collection for just one piece of music. Again, write the copyright owner. Publishers' view differ on this question. Some feel it is a legitimate request and will grant permission to make copies, usually for a fee. Others deny such requests. They reason that no collection will appeal in its entirety to any customer, and if customers can pick and choose from collections at will, the market for collections will be diminished.

Extra parts. In the case of extra parts for bands, publishers recognize that their standard band publications cannot possibly satisfy the instrumentation of every customer. Many publishers adhere to guidelines issued the the American School Band Directors Association or the National Band Association with respect to instrumentation and the number of copies for each part. In addition, many publishers do offer extra parts for sale.

So, first check with your music dealer or the publisher to see if extra parts are available for sale. If so, order them. If you need them immediately you can always make photocopies as a Fair Use while you're waiting for the ordered parts to arrive. But what if the publisher doesn't offer extra parts for sale? Write or ask for permission to make copies. Be specific. Advise which parts you need and how many. A publisher who doesn't offer extra parts had better say yes to this request! But he may quote a fee.

I don't deny that the purchase of extra parts is a significant expense. But the subject is a tough one for publishers, too. Most, I believe, sincerely recognize the band director's problem. In fact a few publishers are experimenting with ways to solve this problem. For example a publisher may include a "license" with each band publication in which the purchaser is granted permission to make photocopies of parts at no charge. Or it may include a form advising the purchaser that he many make photocopies of parts subject to the payment of a small fee. The form must be returned to the publisher along with the fee.

Back in 1984, when I wrote the first edition of this book, I mentioned that I thought we'd see more publishers issuing such photocopying licenses with band publications. But it hasn't really happened. There are a few publishers who do it but the idea hasn't really caught on.

Music for contests. Most contests require that a copy of the student's music be provided to the judges. The rules of many contests prohibit the use of photocopies. No matter how you interpret the law, unauthorized photocopies for judges at contests are copyright infringements. Nevertheless, it does seem odd that a student should purchase two (or three, or four) copies of a solo just to participate in a contest. If you agree, write the publisher and explain the situation.

Personally, I feel this request is a legitimate one, and when I was handling copyright matters for a publisher, I always approved these requests without requiring any fee. Some publishers agree with me; others don't. If a publisher grants you permission to make a copy for a judge, be sure you get it in writing. Some contest judges will accept photocopies only with written permission from the publisher. Check with your contest sponsor or host. And again—don't make copies without permission.

Choral parts or speaking parts for musicals. Do you purchase musicals for your elementary or middle school students to perform? And do you always purchase enough student parts for your students to learn the show? Or do you purchase a few and photocopy the parts for most of your students?

Photocopying parts for musical plays is a blatant violation of copyright and one for which no convincing argument—other than a lack of funds—exists. But lack of funds never justifies photocopying. Cajole your principal for more money, ask the P.T.A. for assistance, or sell candy, but don't copy the parts.

Personally, no other type of unauthorized photocopying bothers me more than this. If I were a music publisher looking to bring a copyright infringement suit against a school, and I needed a situation where there was almost no chance of losing the suit, and where I could demonstrate willful infringement, I would find an elementary or middle school using photocopied parts for a musical. And it wouldn't be hard to find. I'd just look in my file of orders for a purchase order with one score, an accompaniment/performance recording and one student part.

 Photocopying: Classroom and Instructional Use

Music educators do more than just direct bands, orchestras, and choirs. And copyright laws protect more than just music. Plays, novels, poems, graphs, maps, textbooks, photographs, films, stories, and illustrations can all be copyrighted. Abiding by copyright laws means more than just purchasing published copies for your choral group. It means respecting the rights of all copyright owners—not just music publishers.

All copyright owners are afforded the same exclusive rights listed in Chapter 4. The right to make and distribute copies holds for copyright owners of prose works as well as musical works. However, there are Fair Uses for prose works, too.

The criteria for Fair Use, you remember, include (1) the purpose and nature of the use; (2) the nature of the work; (3) the amount or portion of the work used; and (4) the effect of the use upon the potential market for or value of the work.

Just as organizations of music publishers and music educators agreed upon Fair Use guidelines for educational uses of music, organizations of authors and book publishers met with groups representing educational institutions to create Fair Use "Guidelines for Classroom Copying in Not-for-Profit Educational Institutions." Here are those guidelines.

Single Copying for Teachers. A single copy may be made of any of the following by or for a teacher at his or her individual request for his or her scholarly research or use in teaching or preparation for teaching:

- a chapter from a book;

- an article from a periodical or newspaper;

- a short story, short essay or short poem, whether or not from a collective work;

- a chart, graph, diagram, drawing, cartoon or picture from a book, periodical, or newspaper.

Please note that these Fair Uses are for single copies only, for use by teachers only, not students. You may retain these single copies in your file.

Multiple Copies for Classroom Use. Multiple copies (not to exceed in any event more than one copy per pupil in a course) may be made by or for the teacher giving the course for classroom use or discussion; provided that:

- the copying meets the tests of brevity and spontaneity as defined below; *and*

- meets the cumulative effect test as defined below; *and*

- each copy includes a notice of copyright.

Note that Fair Use copies must be both brief *and* spontaneous.

The Fair Use Guidelines then define brevity and spontaneity. The definitions of brevity and spontaneity are very specific and precise so I'll simply reprint them directly from the guidelines.

Definitions

(a) **Brevity**

(i) Poetry: (a) A complete poem if less than 250 words and if printed on not more than two pages or, (b) from a longer poem, an excerpt of not more than 250 words.

(ii) Prose: (a) Either a complete article, story or essay of less than 2,500 words or (b) an excerpt from any prose work of not more than 1,000 words or 10% of the work, whichever is less, but in any event a minimum of 500 words. (Each of the numerical limits stated in (i) and (ii) above may be expanded to permit the completion of an unfinished line of a poem or of an unfinished prose paragraph.)

(iii) Illustration: One chart, graph, diagram, drawing, cartoon or picture per book or periodical issue.

(iv) Special works: Certain works in poetry, prose or in "poetic prose" which often combine language with illustrations and which are intended sometimes for children and at other times for a more general audience fall short of 2,500 words in their entirety. Paragraph (ii) above notwithstanding, such "special works" may not be reproduced in their entirety; however, an excerpt comprising not more than two of the published pages of such special work found in the text thereof, may be reproduced.

b) **Spontaneity**

(i) The copying is at the instance and inspiration of the individual teacher, *and*

(ii) The inspiration and decision to use the work and the moment of its use for maximum teaching effectiveness are so close in time that it would be unreasonable to expect a timely reply to a request for permission.

Remember, *both* requirements must be met to fulfill the spontaneity requirement. The guidelines do not define "a reasonable time period to expect a timely reply."

The Cumulative Effect is defined in four ways:

First, the copying of the material must be for only one course in the school in which the copies are made.

Second, not more than one short poem, article, story, essay or two excerpts may be copied from the same author, and no more than three from the same collective work or periodical volume during one class term. Term is defined as the length of time to complete a course.

Third, there may not be more than nine instances of such multiple copying for one course during one class term.

Finally, no more than three items from the same periodical volume may be copied during one class term.

There is an exception to these Cumulative Effect guidelines, however. Articles from current newspapers, news periodicals, (such as *Newsweek*, *Time*, and others), and the current news sections of other periodicals (such as an article about a recent merger in a business magazine, for example) may be copied. Again, the guidelines fail to define "current" but many independent sources consider two weeks to be "current."

The Fair Use Guidelines specifically prohibit the following:

1. Copying to replace or substitute for anthologies, compilations or collective works. It doesn't matter what sources you use; putting together a collection of articles to create an anthology is expressly prohibited.

2. Copying "consumable" works, which are used in the course of study or teaching. These include workbooks, exercises, standardized tests, test booklets, answer sheets and similar materials.

3. Copying as a substitute for the purchase of books or periodicals.

In addition, the prohibitions state that copying may not be directed by a higher authority. As a teacher, you must feel the spontaneity required in the Fair Use section. If your department chairman suggests copying something for your class, those copies do not meet the Fair Use criteria. It's worth noting, also, that if you should happen to be named as a defendant in a copyright infringement suit, you cannot use the excuse that someone ordered you to do it.

The prohibitions also disallow use of the same item by the same teacher from term to term. In other words, what may be a Fair Use copy used in the Fall term may not be in the Spring term, mainly because in the Spring it fails to meet the spontaneity requirement.

Finally, if Fair Use copies are made and students are charged for those copies, the charge may not exceed the actual cost of the photocopying.

These Fair Uses for Classroom Copying in Not-for-Profit Educational Institutions are fairly complex and specific. Basically, a teacher must be spontaneous in his or her need for multiple photocopies. Today's bright idea used in next semester's Music Appreciation class is hardly a spontaneous use. If you have time to write a copyright owner for the use of his work you must do so. And, under the cumulative effect, you may not make multiple copies of the same material for more than one course.

The remainder of the Fair Uses, especially the tests for brevity are pretty specific and self-explanatory. You can apply them to your own particular situations. Remember that Fair Uses are considered as a group and not individually. The reprinting of a 500 word essay (which is permissible under the test of brevity) would not be a Fair Use if it fails to meet the test of spontaneity or the cumulative effect.

The test of brevity for poetry should not be applied to music lyrics, even if they are under 250 words. Music lyrics are not poetry; they are part of a musical work and thus governed by the Fair Uses for music. *It is not permissible to make copies of copyrighted song lyrics and distribute them to your music classes or choirs for singing unless you obtain permission to do so from the copyright owner.*

Another point on this subject: copyright infringement is copyright infringement, whether it is done with a photocopy machine, a typewriter, or a computer word processing program. The same is true of scanning a text or a musical work, storing it on a disk and then printing it out. Or by the age-old method of hand copying. A few elementary teachers have told me they believe that handwritten or typed copies of song lyrics are not copyright infringements because they are not literally photocopied from a book. They are wrong.

Graphic Works

Although most of this book deals specifically with music and texts, music educators, and in particular, elementary general music teachers should be aware of copyright restrictions related to graphics. Graphics includes paintings, photographs, maps, diagrams, charts, posters, and cartoon characters.

Fair Uses for graphic works are similar to those of prose works. Further, a teacher may make multiple copies of a graphic work for classroom use provided that:

- The copy is made at the inspiration of the teacher (not ordered or suggested by someone else), and is so close to the required use that writing for permission is impossible.

- The copy is used in one course only.

- There are no more than nine instances of multiple copying for that course.

- No more than one graphic work is copied from any book or periodical.

You may make a single copy of any graphic work for your own reference, study, or research.

Adaptations of graphic works, like arrangements of musical works, move into another area, and one which copyright owners of graphic works frown upon. Be aware also that large corporations such as Disney and Warner Bros. are on the lookout for unauthorized uses of their cartoon characters. Scanning or copying a Warner Bros. cartoon character without permission and using it graphically on, say, a band T-shirt, would be a copyright infringement and most likely a trademark infringement as well.

 *Recordings*

One of the most important exclusive rights afforded to copyright owners of musical works is the right "to reproduce the copyrighted work in copies or phonorecords." A musical composition does not exist only on paper; it exists also when it is performed and recorded. So a song can be copied in two ways. It can be notated on paper or it can be recorded. Under the Copyright Act of 1976, copyright owners have the exclusive right to record as well as to print copies.

History of the Recording Right

Prior to the invention of the phonograph, music publishers earned most of their income from the sale of printed music. Between 1900 and 1910, for example, over 100 songs sold more than one million copies of sheet music. But times were changing.

The invention of the player piano and piano rolls in the 1880's caused a stir in the music world. Piano rolls were the first widely accepted means of recording a song. For the first time a non-musician of modest financial means could enjoy music in his own home. All he needed was a player piano and some piano rolls. This was truly a technological revolution. Piano roll manufacturers recognized copyright in musical works and music publishers began granting licenses for the "mechanical reproduction" of their songs on piano rolls. The manufacturers were willing to pay large sums for licenses to record popular hit songs. And if a manufacturer could obtain the exclusive right to record a big hit he would pay even more. Since he had the only piano roll of that song he could naturally charge more, too. By 1909, one large company, the Aeolian Piano Roll Company, was monopolizing the industry by paying huge fees for "exclusive" piano roll recordings.

The mechanical right was the most hotly contested issue in the debate over the Copyright Act of 1909. Congress didn't deny that copyright owners had the right to grant licenses for recordings for their songs, but on the other hand, Congress didn't like one company monopolizing an entire industry. Further, it felt that the public was not well served when only one piano roll recording of a popular song could be marketed. The compromise contained in the Act of 1909 was the "Compulsory Mechanical License" (also called the "Statutory Mechanical License").

The Compulsory Mechanical License stated that once a copyright owner had recorded a song for public distribution, or had granted permission to someone else to do so, anyone could record that song by following certain procedures which included the payment of a royalty of 2¢ per recording to the copyright owner. Thus, a copyright owner could control the first recording of his work, but thereafter the work could be recorded by anyone willing to pay the 2¢ royalty per recording.

Although music publishers at first opposed the Compulsory Mechanical License, they grew to love it decades later when the phonograph replaced the piano roll and recordings sold by the millions. Each copy sold meant 2¢ for the publisher, and the composer usually got half of that. By the 1950's and 1960's recordings of popular music were pumping millions of dollars in mechanical royalties into publishers' and songwriters' pockets. The mechanical royalty was still fixed, by law, at 2¢ per song per recording, just as it had been in 1909. But no one seemed to care; business was booming.

When Congress began considering a new copyright law to

replace the Act of 1909, the Compulsory Mechanical License came under close scrutiny. (Incidentally, the name "mechanical license" stuck, even though hardly anyone refers to tapes, CD's, or even vinyl records as "mechanical recordings" these days.) Ultimately Congress decided to keep most elements of the Compulsory Mechanical License in the Act of 1976. They did, however, agree to raise the required royalty from 2¢ to 2 $^3/4$¢ or $^1/2$¢ per minute of playing time, whichever is greater. Further, the rate would be reviewed periodically by the Copyright Royalty Tribunal, a panel established to review royalty rates on the numerous compulsory licenses (not all music-related, by the way) in the Act of 1976.

Although the Copyright Royalty Tribunal no longer exists, increases in compulsory royalties continue to be subject to revision under the jurisdiction of the Copyright Office. Each review involves negotiation between copyright owners and users and the approval of the Copyright Office. As of January 1, 1998 the compulsory mechanical royalty stands at:

> *7.1¢ per musical work or 1.35¢ per minute of playing time, whichever is greater.*

Undoubtedly revisions will be made in the future. To get the current, up to date rate, check The Harry Fox Agency website (listed in the Glossary). Remember, the rate remained unchanged at 2¢ per song per recording from 1909 until January 1, 1978 (the date the Copyright Act of 1976 took effect) when it increased to 2 $^3/4$¢.

A few points must be made about the mechanical royalty rate. First, under the 1976 Act, the rate pertains to each recording "made and distributed." A copy distributed free of charge is not by law exempt from royalty payment. Second, the rate pertains to each musical work contained on a recording. Thus, a cassette containing two songs—one on each side—has two royalty obligations, a CD with ten songs has ten royalty obligations, and so on.

Third, "mechanical recordings" pertain to any type of device used to reproduce music, such as CD's, cassettes, vinyl records, music boxes, MIDI disks (at least those which can be played only in audio format), and yes, even piano rolls. Finally, the rates established by statute are the maximum rates that a copyright owner may charge for the use of his musical work on a recording. There is nothing to prevent the copyright owner and a user such as a recording company from negotiating a lower rate. In fact, in the commercial music industry negotiated rates are a part of doing business.

A quick note about MIDI disks. Most, but not all, music publishers consider MIDI disks no different than any other audio recording if the disk can be played in audio format only. But if the disk contains other computer code which, for example, can print out the music, then the compulsory mechanical royalty would not apply and a separate fee would have to be negotiated between the copyright owner and the MIDI disk producer. Computer CD-ROMs which contain visual images would not be not be covered by the compulsory mechanical license.

Fair Uses

How does all this pertain to music education? First of all, there are two important Fair Use limitations on the right to record.

(1) A single copy of a sound recording (such as a tape, disc or cassette) of copyrighted music may be made from sound recordings owned by an educational institution or an individual teacher for the purpose of constructing aural exercises or examinations and may be retained by the educational institution or individual teacher.

Just as the photocopying of music is a copyright infringement, so is the copying of recordings. Both popular and serious music publishers lose millions of dollars each year in sales lost to unauthorized copies of recordings. This practice is literally no different than photocopying printed music. However, this Fair Use allows music educators to copy recordings *solely for exercises or examinations.*

(2) A single copy of recordings of performance by students may be made for evaluation and rehearsal purposes and may be retained by the educational institution or individual teacher.

This Fair Use seems self-explanatory and logical. You needn't bother with the nickels and dimes which would otherwise be due on such recordings. A common example would be a single recording of a private student or a performing group, provided the recording is made solely for evaluating student or group progress. Obviously, if you record a choral or band concert and sell copies of the recording, this Fair Use doesn't apply.

Recording Your Performing Group

Suppose you *do* want to record your band, orchestra, choir, or show choir, and you want to sell copies of the recording. First of all, even if the recording is not made "for profit," it is still subject to payment of the mechanical royalty. The compulsory mechanical royalty is due on all recordings "made and distributed." So a recording sold solely to raise funds for a choir tour or new tuba is not exempt from payment of royalties.

You pay a recording engineer, you pay the CD or cassette

manufacturers. You may even pay a recording studio. So don't you think that the publisher who owns the copyright (and who in turn pays the composer) deserves to be paid too? Without the publisher and composer there would be nothing to record.

"But I've already paid for the music when I bought it," you may say. "Now I'm expected to pay again, just to record it?" Yes. "Isn't that a rip-off?" No.

When you purchase a printed copy you become the owner of a piece of paper containing some printed symbols. You may also have some rights to perform the piece of music which I'll discuss in the next chapter. But the right to perform and the right to record are two separate and distinct rights. If you want to make a recording and distribute copies, you are required to pay the compulsory mechanical royalty as required by the Act of 1976. The fact that you are an educator and not Sony makes no difference.

Under the terms of the Compulsory Mechanical License, a copyright owner (which is usually, but not always, the publisher) cannot, after the first recording of a musical work, prohibit any subsequent recordings. So you don't have to worry about getting permission to record—assuming the work has been previously recorded and you're prepared to pay a royalty. Nevertheless, your first step should be a letter to the copyright owner before you record and request a license to record the work. In the event the work has never been recorded the copyright owner does have the option of denying your request but chances are he would grant you a license anyway. Most music publishers and composers are usually happy to have their works recorded.

The copyright owner will then issue you a license to record the work and you may proceed with the recording. Actually, if you're prepared to pay the required royalty there is no need to wait until you receive the license before making the recording.

For commercial recordings, many publishers use the services of an agent who specializes in handling mechanical licenses. The agent collects all income on licenses issued on behalf of the publisher and periodically audits the books of record companies, recouping royalties which otherwise may be lost to the publisher. In return, the agent receives a small commission on all he collects for the publisher.

Some publishers use the services of such an agent for small recordings made by schools and churches. Others issue their licenses directly. The most widely used agent is The Harry Fox Agency, Inc., in New York City. If you're planning a recording project with several songs, one letter or phone call to the Fox Agency may save a lot of time. Their address and phone number are listed in the Glossary. Chances are the Fox Agency represents many of the publishers involved in your project and can issue licenses on their behalf. When you contact the Fox Agency, be sure you correctly list the title, writer, and copyright owner of the works you plan to record. In fact, it's a good idea to list the titles and writers even when writing directly to copyright owners.

Whether you obtain a license directly from a copyright owner or from his agent, follow the instructions outlined in the license.

Some Questions Concerning Recordings

Suppose I hire a recording company to record my group. Shouldn't the recording company pay the royalties? Actually, it doesn't matter who pays the royalties as long as someone does. Some recording companies may offer to obtain licenses for you and pay all royalties. The cost of the royalties will probably be included somewhere in your invoice so you're really not getting a bargain. But having the recording company handle the paperwork will save you a lot of time. If the recording company doesn't offer to handle the mechanical royalties it's up to you to do so. In any event, make sure you discuss the matter of royalties with your recording company. Ultimately you, as the "producer" of the recording are responsible for the royalties. You can't get off the hook by saying, "I thought the recording company took care of it."

Suppose I'm giving away the recording or I'm selling it to raise funds for a truly worthy cause. Do I still have to pay the full royalty? If you really feel your situation justifies a waiver of royalties, write the copyright owner and ask if he will waive payment of mechanical royalties or if he will accept a reduced rate. (Remember, he can never charge you more than the compulsory royalty rate.) Some publishers will. Others won't and will cite the argument that the CD or cassette manufacturer gets paid, so he should be paid, too.

What if I don't know who owns the copyright on the composition I want to record? Or what if I can't locate the copyright owner? It's really your responsibility to try to locate copyright owners. But sometimes, as I know from personal experience, it's difficult, if not impossible. If you have a published copy of the composition, the copyright owner will be identified in the copyright notice at the bottom of the first page of music. Often, however, no address is shown in the copyright notice. Or sometimes the ownership of the work has changed and the copyright notice identifies a previous owner.

There are several sources, such as your music dealer, for tracking down copyright owners. The performing rights organizations, ASCAP and BMI, can help, too. (I'll talk more about them in the next chapter.) So can The Harry Fox Agency. All three have websites with searchable databases of musical works to help you track down titles. If all else fails there's the Copyright Office in Washington, DC. See the Glossary for addresses.

In writing to such organizations, you'll need correct and complete titles and writer information. If you don't have at least that information you'll really have problems tracking down a copyright owner. If you've exhausted every possible avenue and still can't locate the copyright owner, I'd suggest you go ahead and make the recording anyway and set aside any royalties you should pay on the musical work. That way, if anyone ever claims copyright in the work you'll have the money to pay them.

What about recordings made at festivals? They're not exempt from the payment of mechanical royalties. The festival organizers or the organization sponsoring the festival is responsible for the payment of such royalties. Remember, just because a recording is not-for-profit doesn't mean it is exempt from paying royalties. And even though the festival itself may be "non-profit," that doesn't mean the recording company is doing it for nothing. They're getting paid, so why shouldn't the composers?

8 Performances

The right of public performance is the most misunderstood and complex of the five exclusive rights granted to copyright owners of musical works. Some people find it hard to believe that musical works are not free to be performed by anyone, at any time, and under any circumstances. But in fact, the 1976 Copyright Act clearly states that the copyright owner of a musical work has the exclusive right to perform the copyrighted work publicly.

However, Congress recognized that limiting performances exclusively to copyright owners would not serve the public. So the 1976 Act has a long list of limitations—Fair Uses—on the public performance right. Such Fair Use performances are called "exempt performances." Most musical performances made by public school and college performing groups are exempt performances.

History of the Public Performance Right

The concept of performing rights was first applied to dramatic works such as plays and operettas by European countries in the nineteenth century. Before public performance rights were recognized there was extensive pirating of dramatic works. It was not uncommon to find several competing productions of a popular play. Naturally, the unauthorized productions took business away from the playwright's own production but the playwright and his producer were powerless to do anything about it. Most European countries recognized the playwright's problem and granted the copyright owner of a dramatic work the exclusive right to perform the work. Just as an unauthorized publication of a novel constituted a copyright infringement, now an unauthorized performance of a play was also an infringement. Eventually the right of public performance was extended to musical works as well.

The United States, however, did not grant the right of public performance to copyright owners of dramatic and musical works until 1897. During the nineteenth century, piracy of plays was widespread in this country. For example, when Britain's Gilbert and Sullivan exported productions of their popular operettas to the United States, American producers purchased quantities of opening night seats for stenographers who transcribed the dialog. With a legally purchased copy of the musical score and a transcribed dialog, a producer could have his own production of a Gilbert and Sullivan show on stage within weeks—and without any payment to Gilbert and Sullivan. All of this was quite legal until 1897. (Imagine Andrew Lloyd Webber tolerating this today!)

Music publishers, believing that public performance of songs increased sheet music sales, at first ignored their right to public performance and encouraged all performances of their works. In 1909, Congress recognized that even though music publishers were not taking advantage of the public performance right, they could conceivably restrict all performances of a musical work. Theoretically, anyone who performed a song without permission from the copyright owner was a copyright infringer. Congress had visions of school children fined for singing in the classroom or churchgoers prohibited from singing hymns. It never happened, of course, but under existing law it was possible.

So Congress significantly modified the performance right in the 1909 Act and limited the right of public performance to performances made "for profit." School children and churchgoers were safe! But ballrooms, restaurants and night clubs which hired bands for the entertainment of their patrons were not. The Supreme Court ruled that the performance of music in such establishments—even if no admission was charged—was a "for profit" use.

In 1914, a group of publishers, composers, and songwriters organized the American Society of Composers, Authors and Publishers (ASCAP) for the sole purpose of exercising their right of public performance. In time, with the invention of radio and television, the right to control public performances resulted in considerable income for publishers and composers. Performing rights organizations such as ASCAP made it all possible.

I'll pick up ASCAP's history and the role of performing rights organizations later in this chapter. But first...

The Public Performance Right and the Act of 1976

The Copyright Act of 1976 eliminated the "for profit" limitation on the public performance right. Today "non-profit" no longer guarantees immunity from a copyright owner's right to control performance of his work. Are we back to where we started? Are school children and churchgoers in peril again? No.

Congress eliminated the "for profit" limitation but added nine new and specific limitations. Performances of music under the following circumstances are exempt performances and are not copyright infringements.

(1) Face-to-face teaching activities in a non-profit educational institution;

(2) Instructional broadcasting (broadcasts that are essentially an adjunct to actual classwork of educational institutions as opposed to public broadcasts which are directed to the public at large);

(3) Religious services;

(4) Live performances without commercial advantage to anyone;

(5) Reception of broadcasts in a public place;

(6) Annual agricultural and horticultural fairs;

(7) Public performance in connection with sale of recordings or sheet music;

(8) Non-Commercial broadcasts to the blind or deaf;

(9) Non-profit performances of dramatic works transmitted to the blind by radio subcarrier.

Limitations (1) and (4) cover most live performances of music by school performing groups.

Limitations (5) and (6) are interesting. Limitation (5) protects anyone from liability for simply turning on a radio or television in a public place. And the lobbyists for state fairs did their job with the sixth limitation. It's a good example of the democratic process—a tiny but powerful special interest group at work.

Performances in Face-to-Face Teaching Situations

Most performances of music in classroom situations are exempt performances. To be exempt, the performance must be made by an instructor or pupil in the course of face-to-face teaching activities of a non-profit educational institution, in a classroom or similar place devoted to instruction.

Incidentally, performances need not be "live" to be copyright infringements. Playing a recording of a pop song in your general music class is a performance, though it is exempt under the face-to-face teaching limitations. Playing recordings under other situations may not be exempt.

Live Performances Without Commercial Advantage to Anyone

Most performances of music by your school's performing groups are exempt under this limitation. Note that the limitation does not say "non-profit" performances; it says "performances without commercial advantage to anyone." There is a difference. The law is specific in describing such performances. Under the terms of this limitation, a live performance of a musical work is "without commercial advantage to anyone..."

- if no payments are made to any performers, promoters, or organizers; *and*

- if there is no direct or indirect admission charge.

If an admission is charged the performance is still exempt if the proceeds (after deducting reasonable costs for producing the performance) are used exclusively for educational, religious, or charitable purposes.

However, in spite of all this, a copyright owner may prohibit performance of his work by serving notice at least seven days before the performance. This "limitation on the limitation" enables a copyright owner to prohibit a performance of his work. Congress intended it to be used in circumstances where, for example, a copyright owner objects to the "educational, religious, or charitable purpose" served by a performance or concert involving his work. It is not clear how a copyright owner can possibly be aware of all upcoming performances of his work by educational, religious, or charitable groups. There is no requirement for a performer or promoter to notify the copyright owner of a work. For practical purposes, educators need not be concerned about a copyright owner prohibiting the performance of music educational concerts (unless you're raising money, say, to promote global warming and advertise it in *USA Today*).

Clearly, most concerts by school performing groups are exempt under this limitation. However, your performance, technically, might not be exempt if, for example, you hired and paid a guest soloist to perform at the concert—even if the admission charge paid the soloist's fee.

The "live performances without commercial advantage" limitation covers only non-dramatic literary and musical works. Performance of dramatic works such as plays, musical plays, operas and operettas are not exempt. From a technical standpoint, then, if you're performing an elementary musical play you should contact the copyright owner about performance fees—even if you are not charging admission.

I continue to say "technically" and "from a technical standpoint" because, as a practical matter, most publishers of elementary musicals are not concerned about collecting performance fees for the performance of their musicals. You simply shouldn't worry about it. On the other hand, I want to make you aware of the law in this area of educational music. But just because a copyright owner has the right to do something (in this case, collect performance fees for the performance of elementary musicals) doesn't mean he's going to exercise that right. And most publishers of elementary musicals don't.

But some may require the purchase of a certain number of parts for performance and you should understand that this is simply a means of insuring that you have purchased a minimum requirement as set by the publisher. In reality, the rights involved in presenting an elementary musical are no different than those involved with a high school performance of *The Music Man*. And anyone who has presented a school performance of a Broadway musical knows how fussy the licensing agents are about their musicals.

"But there's a difference," you may say. "Parts for *The Music Man* are available only on rental. Naturally we expect to pay a performance fee. But I've purchased copies of the elementary musical. Our school owns the parts. Doesn't that give us the right to perform?"

No. Remember that when you purchase a copy of a piece of music you simply own the copy. You do not purchase any rights in the music.

The Act of 1976 makes a distinction between a non-dramatic work, such as a piece of choral music, and a dramatic work, such as a musical play. When you purchase a piece of choral music you do not purchase the right to perform. However, you are free to perform the work under the specific exempt situations listed in this chapter. Dramatic works do not enjoy as many limitations on performance as do musical works.

The only limitation on the performance of dramatic works is in face-to-face teaching situations. Performances of musical plays "without commercial advantage to anyone" are not exempt. Many publishers who sell their musicals (as opposed to renting them) list their performance requirements, if any, in the scores of their musicals. Abide by those requirements. If you are in doubt, contact the publisher *before* you select a musical play for your elementary students.

So, once again, with respect to the specific rights involved, there is no difference between a school performance of *The Music Man* and your fifth grade musical. There is, however, a great difference in the way the owners of these works approach their public performance right. Don't worry about it, just be aware of it.

This discussion of the rights involved in musicals brings me to another, related subject—one that I did not cover in the first edition of this book because I was not aware that it was prevalent. But since then I've had several music educators ask me about their practice of performing scenes from a musical or a greatly condensed version of a show by purchasing a copy of the show's score and a published choral medley (or by using copies of the score). By doing this you've moved well beyond the purview of face-to-face performances of musical works in an educational setting and well into the area of performance rights in dramatic works. Plus, you've "adapted" the musical without the copyright owner's permission.

This is a blatant infringement of several of the rights of the copyright owner of the musical play. And it happens to be in an area where the copyright owners are very protective of their rights, and very litigious. If the owner of a musical discovers you are doing this to one of his musicals you can count on a very nasty "cease and desist" letter, at the very least, and quite possibly a significant copyright infringement suit. It is in the strongest possible terms that I urge you not to do this.

Non-Exempt Performances in Educational Institutions

Performances of music under the following circumstances are not exempt performances in schools and colleges, whether private or public, because all involve paid performers:

- Concerts by paid performers such as rock, jazz or country bands
- School dances using live bands or deejays
- Orchestras in residence
- Concerts by touring performing groups
- School assemblies featuring outside, paid performers
- Background music in school buildings

Please note that most of the non-exempt musical performances in schools and colleges do not involve performances by music department groups. The vast majority of performances made by school ensembles are exempt under limitations (1) and (4) of the public performance right.

What should you do if there are non-exempt performances of music in your school? Here's where performing rights organizations enter the picture.

Performing Rights Organizations

Back in 1914, after the Supreme Court ruled that live musical performances in ballrooms, restaurants, and night clubs were "for profit" and thus not exempt from the performance right, the ballroom, restaurant, and night club owners obviously had many questions. And the American Society of Composers, Authors, and

Publishers had the answers. The ballroom, restaurant, and night club owners had two choices: they could negotiate with the copyright owner of every musical work performed in their establishments or they could purchase a "blanket" license to perform all the works written or published by ASCAP's members.

Naturally, most chose the ASCAP blanket license because it was simpler. ASCAP, in turn, distributed the fees from the purchase of performing licenses to its members. And that's still what ASCAP does today; it offers blanket performing licenses to users of music and distributes this income to its members.

Things are more complicated today, though. For one thing, there are two other performing rights organizations in the United States. Broadcast Music, Inc. (BMI) was founded in 1939 by a group of broadcasters who felt there should be a competitive alternative to ASCAP, and who wanted to create a repertory of songs to compete with the ASCAP repertory. They succeeded, and today ASCAP and BMI are nearly equal in size. BMI has more writer members but ASCAP still collects a bit more money than BMI. A third, much smaller performing rights organization is SESAC (which originally stood for the Society of European Stage Authors and Composers). ASCAP and BMI collect over 99 percent of the performing rights income in the United States. SESAC gets the rest.

The users of music have changed considerably since 1914, too. Night clubs and restaurants still purchase blanket license to perform music (though in any given year there are usually a few bills floating around Congress supported by small business owners which would exempt small businesses from paying any fees to performing rights organizations). But today the bulk of the income for performing rights organizations comes from television and radio. Broadcasters purchase performing rights licenses from ASCAP, BMI, and SESAC, and in return they may perform any music written or published by an ASCAP, BMI, or SESAC member. All three have reciprocal agreements with performing rights organizations in countries around the world so a broadcaster holding ASCAP, BMI, and SESAC licenses can perform or broadcast virtually every piece of copyrighted music in the world. Imagine the problems associated with tracking down the copyright owner of every song a television network wanted to broadcast. Licenses from performing rights organizations make life a lot easier for broadcasters.

The fees charged broadcasters by BMI and ASCAP are pegged to a percentage of the broadcaster's advertising revenue and are continually monitored and subject to review by federal judges. Throughout ASCAP and BMI's history, broadcasters have grumbled about fees for performing rights licenses and have even questioned their legality. However, courts have consistently upheld the legality of the blanket performing license. The issue usually boils down to money; broadcasters would like to get music for free and, if they can't get it for free, then they'd like to get it for less than they're currently paying. Broadcasters still have the option of dealing directly with copyright owners and as an ASCAP writer member, my agreement with ASCAP is non-exclusive, which means I am free to deal directly with a broadcaster if I wish. But direct negotiation of fees between a broadcaster and a composer is extremely rare.

I don't know how ASCAP distributed its income to its members in 1914, but today it takes a small army of economists, mathematicians, consultants, and judges armed with computers, diaries, logs, and regional issues of *TV Guide*. In theory, a composer should earn some performance income each time his work is broadcast. In reality, it's impossible for the performing rights organizations to monitor every single minute of broadcast time in the United States. ASCAP and BMI do, however, take a complete census of all music performed on network television and major cable networks. (That's where *TV Guide* comes in.)

For local television and radio stations, ASCAP and BMI monitor a sampling of broadcasts and log all the music performed during those sample broadcasts. Such performances are called surveyed performances. The more a radio or television station pays in fees, the more often it is monitored. At the end of a quarterly period, the licensing organization recounts all the surveyed performances which are then "weighted" according to the source and time of the performance. A prime-time network performance receives more weight than a 3:00 a.m. broadcast on a small radio station in Boise, Idaho, for example. The amount of money received during the quarter is then allocated among the owners of the weighted, surveyed works and distributed on the basis of 50% to the publisher and 50% to the writer(s) of each work.

Incidentally, Public Broadcasters, which were exempt under the "non-profit" aspect of the 1909 Act, are no longer exempt under the "no commercial advantage to anyone" limitation of the 1976 Act.

Performance rights organizations license other users of music as well. Some other licensees include: night clubs, restaurants, bars and taverns, background music services such as Muzak, arenas, stadiums, auditoriums, concert promoters, convention and trade shows, circuses, ice shows, orchestras, dance studios, and even licensed performances on the internet.

Schools and Colleges and Performing Rights Organizations

Because most schools are "non-profit" institutions, they were exempt from the performance right under the Act of 1909.

The Act of 1976 changed that. Except for the specific exemptions noted in this chapter, performances in schools are no longer automatically exempt from the public performance right. However, at this time neither performing rights organization is involved in blanket licensing of public or private secondary or elementary schools. There may be specific instances, though, where ASCAP or BMI may contact a public or private school about a single use license. For example, let's say the band boosters are presenting a concert of a touring, professional jazz band, or a country singer, in the school auditorium, with the funds used to raise money for the school band. In such case, the organization may be obligated to obtain a single performance license for the concert, especially if the concert promoter doesn't have a blanket license.

In the late 1970's, ASCAP and BMI began licensing colleges and universities and today well over 90% of all U.S. institutions of higher learning have performing rights licenses. The cost is minimal; ASCAP's fee is presently less than 20¢ per student per year.

Let me emphasize that there are scores of uses of music on college campuses and most are not affiliated with the music department. Blanket performance licenses from ASCAP and BMI cover virtually all of them, including:

- all concert performances
- dances or parties (whether with live or recorded music) hosted by the college and/or its social organizations
- athletic events
- background music used in school cafeterias or campus stores
- music used "on hold" in telephone systems

The licenses do not cover:

- Campus radio stations. They require a separate license.

- Off-campus performances by school groups not engaged by the school. Examples would be a marching band performance at a bowl game or a choir performance at a concert hall while on tour. In both cases, however, it's quite possible that the promoters of the event have performing rights licenses.

- Performances of dramatic works such as musicals or operas. In such cases a performance fee is usually negotiated directly with the copyright owner or its agent when the scores are rented or purchased.

- Permission to make arrangements of copyrighted works made by students or faculty. I mention this only because some college instructors have told me that because their school has an ASCAP license, they believe they may arrange any song in the ASCAP repertoire without permission from anyone. This is false.

As a music department faculty member, your only requirement may be to submit copies of any available concert programs to ASCAP and BMI. You don't need to fill out any forms or prepare anything special; copies of the programs prepared for distribution at the event are satisfactory. It may be a minor nuisance but the programs are used to ensure proper distribution of royalties to ASCAP and BMI composers. Think of it as another way to support the creation of music for educational use. The money is paid by your administration for the use of *all* music performed on campus. By submitting concert programs you insure that at least some of that money is paid to the creators of the works you perform.

Your role, as a music educator, in the matter of performing rights in music, should be to educate your students and your administration and help them understand the concept of performing rights. Stress both the moral and legal aspects. I assume that *you* support the concept of copyright and payment for creators of musical works. Morally, music departments should lead the fight for adherence to copyright laws.

Broadcast Performances

Suppose one of your performing groups has the opportunity to perform on radio or television, either broadcast television or cable. It's really the responsibility of the broadcaster to obtain clearance for the broadcast of music. So nearly all radio stations, television stations, and cable companies have blanket licenses from the performing rights organizations. If asked, simply provide the broadcaster with the titles, writers, and copyright owners of the works you plan to perform. The broadcaster should take care of the rest. If you know the performing rights affiliation of the copyright owner (ASCAP or BMI), provide that information, too.

Performing rights organizations only license performances of music. They do not license dramatic works such as musical plays. For permission to broadcast a musical play you or the broadcaster must contact the copyright owner of the work, even if the broadcaster has licenses from ASCAP and BMI. Many copyright owners of musicals will expect a performance fee. The broadcaster might agree to pay the fee but if not, payment of the fee would then be your responsibility...that is, if you're determined to see your students on television.

9 *Arrangements*

At one time or another, you've probably done some arranging for your students. Most music educators do. Perhaps you couldn't find a suitable choral arrangement of a particular pop song for your group. Or maybe you just wanted to brush up on some arranging skills which had rusted since your college theory classes. In any case, the question of copyright must be considered before you make your arrangement.

Any arrangement of a copyrighted musical work made without permission of the copyright owner is a copyright infringement. That's a pretty blunt statement but it's reality. There are no Fair uses for arranging.

One of the exclusive rights granted to copyright owners is "the right to prepare derivative works based on the copyrighted work." A derivative work is any adaptation of a copyrighted work. A motion picture or television drama adapted from a novel or a short story is a derivative work. So is a Broadway musical based on a play. A transfer from one medium to another, such as a screenplay adapted from a play, is also a derivative work.

In the field of music, derivative works include the following:

- Arrangements
- Transcriptions
- Simplified editions
  (such as E-Z or big note piano arrangements)
- Adaptations
- Translations of texts
- Orchestrations
- Instrumental accompaniments to piano/vocal works

The copyright owner, alone, has the right to make such derivative works.

So if you want to arrange, adapt, simplify, edit, or translate a copyrighted work, ask for permission before you do it.

How to Obtain Permission to Make an Arrangement

First, identify and locate the copyright owner. The copyright notice at the bottom of the first page of music on any printed copy will give you the name of the owner. Sometimes the credits on a CD label or liner will, too. Or you can contact ASCAP or BMI, but only if you have accurate title and writer information. ASCAP and BMI can give you addresses of publishers, too. Check their searchable databases of musical works on their websites. Their website URL's are listed in the Glossary.

Be sure to check the copyright date. If you can determine that the work is in the Public Domain you don't need any permission to make an arrangement.

If the work is protected by copyright, your next step, then, is to contact the copyright owner and request permission to make an arrangement of the work. A letter, fax or e-mail is better than a phone call. Be specific and provide as much information as possible.

- What kind of arrangement do you want to make? Marching band? Choral? Flute trio?

- How many copies or parts will you make?

- Will you be making the arrangement or will you be paying someone else to do it?

- Who will be performing the arrangement? Your band? Another band?

- Do you propose to sell the arrangement? If so, why, and what will be the approximate selling price?

- Is the arrangement for one specific occasion, such as a graduation ceremony, or will it become a part of your group's repertoire?

The more information you can provide, the better your chances of getting a speedy reply. A publisher needs such information so he can make a decision on whether or not to grant permission to make the arrangement and if so, whether or not to charge a fee.

When I was handling requests such as these for an educational publisher I got many requests to arrange with too little information such as, "Please give me permission to make an orchestral arrangement of (one of our songs). Thank you." This request doesn't provide nearly enough information for me to make an appropriate reply on behalf of the publisher.

What does this person propose to do with the arrangement? Does he plan to sell it? If so, then I definitely want to charge a fee? Is it for a middle school orchestra in rural Missouri, or for performance by a major metropolitan orchestra? The answer to this question would also determine any fee I might charge. I would have to follow up and ask many of the pertinent questions I listed above before I could grant permission.

So be as specific as possible and don't attempt to hide anything from the copyright owner or publisher. If you do, chances are you'll be asked for more information.

A copyright owner has no obligation to grant permission to make arrangements. Courts have confirmed this. If you want to make an SAB choral arrangement of a piece and the publisher has one in print and available for sale he might deny your request. If, however, he finds your request reasonable, a copyright owner will grant permission to arrange. Sometimes he will charge a fee, usually depending on how you propose to use the arrangement, and sometimes not.

If permission is granted, be sure you get something in writing. Don't rely on someone's OK over the phone. You'll be required to show a copyright notice, as prescribed by the copyright owner, on your arrangement. This notice must be placed on all copies, including, in the case of instrumental works, on the score and all parts.

If you are denied permission to make an arrangement, *don't make the arrangement*. You're really setting yourself up for a copyright infringement suit if you do.

Several pop music publishers have successfully sued jazz and marching band arrangers who openly sold unauthorized arrangements. Publishers consider the sale of unauthorized arrangements a willful and serious infringement. Courts have fined some arrangers over $40,000 in penalties and damages in such cases. If you are selling unauthorized arrangements of pop songs I strongly urge you to stop immediately. And you'd better destroy any ads, promotional information or price lists which may be floating around. They can easily fall into a publisher's hands and be used as evidence against you.

Placing ads for the sale of unauthorized arrangements or even advertising your services as a pop or custom arranger arranger is like raising a red flag. Believe me, someone will see it and bring it to the attention of the publishers whose works you are arranging. And if you're buying custom arrangements, be forewarned that unless your arranger has gotten approval for his arrangement you're probably buying an infringing arrangement.

Other Derivative Works

Adaptations. I never really know what someone means when he asks if he may "adapt" a piece of music. The term means different things to different people. An "adaptation" can mean anything from a full blown orchestration to altering a few notes in the tenor part of a choral work.

Technically, you must ask for permission to adapt a musical work in any way. As a practical matter, though, I realize it's a nuisance to write a publisher for permission to change a few notes in a tenor part. And most music publishers probably don't want to be inundated with such requests either, although some are providing information relating to copyright on their websites. So let's consider Fair Uses.

One Fair Use indeed covers adaptations: printed copies which have been purchased may be edited or simplified, provided that the fundamental character of the work is not distorted or the lyrics, if any, are altered, or lyrics added if none exist. In addition, the general principle of Fair Use can help to determine whether or not you ought to request permission to "adapt" a work. Two of the four factors used in determining Fair Use are "the amount and substantiality of the portion used in relation to the copyrighted work as a whole" and "the effect of the use upon the potential market for or value of the copyrighted work." In other words, how much are you adapting it and will the adaptation affect the value or sales of the work?

So assuming you've purchased a sufficient quantity of a choral work for your SATB choir, changing a few notes in the tenor line wouldn't be a problem. But suppose you have a single copy of a 2-part work and you want to adapt it for your SATB choir by writing out men's parts, notesetting it with your Finale software program, and distributing copies to your male singers.

Now we're talking a major adaptation. If the publisher already has an SATB version in print, he might consider this adaptation (from 2-part to SATB) as a possible loss of sales for his SATB edition.

Let's consider the rule of thumb: What if everyone did it? If everyone bought a single copy of the 2-part edition and adapted it for SATB, no copies of the SATB edition would be sold. That's theoretical, of course, but it might be a reason why a publisher would consider this adaptation to be outside the limits of Fair Use and thus a copyright infringement.

Case in point: a friend of mine used to tell me about his church choral director who, even though he had a large choir, insisted on using SAB editions he made himself of published SATB choral works. Both of us were pretty sure the only reason he did this was because he didn't want to spend any money on music. After all, there are thousands of SAB pieces in print. Why then, did he perform only adaptations of SATB works for which no SAB editions were available? He considered them Fair Use adaptations, but they are not.

To summarize, *any adaptation which results in a lost sale to the publisher or which alters the character of the work definitely requires permission from the copyright owner.* Instrumental accompaniments to vocal or choral works also require permission.

Transcriptions. Before transcribing a copyrighted work or arrangement from one medium to another (for example, transcribing an organ work for brass quintet) you must obtain permission from the copyright owner of the work. Please note: arrangements of Public Domain works are copyrightable. You may not adapt or orchestrate a copyrighted arrangement of such a work without permission, even if the basic work is in the Public Domain. Thus you would need permission to do a handbell transcription of a published, simplified arrangement of a Mozart piano sonata.

Parody lyrics, altered texts and translations. Parody lyrics are lyrics which replace the original lyrics of a vocal work or are added to an instrumental work. For example, the senior class members of your choir have written new words to *Proud to be an American* and propose to sing it at their graduation.

In general, any parody lyric or the revision of a lyric that changes the integrity of the work requires authorization from the copyright owner. Altering just a few words in a text is another matter. Suppose you want to change just the last text line in a song to personalize it for your group. As a practical matter, and assuming again that you've bought a sufficient number of copies for your group, I'd say go ahead and do it. (I always say "assuming you've bought a sufficient number of copies for your group" because if you haven't, then it's difficult for you to claim a Fair Use exemption.) To be extra safe, ask for permission, and chances are you'll get it.

Translating a copyrighted text requires permission from the copyright owner of the text. So does taking a copyrighted text and setting it to music.

10 *Videos*

The producers, writers, and creators of motion pictures, videos, and television programs enjoy many of the same rights accorded to musical composers and publishers. Some of those rights include the right to reproduce the work, the right of public distribution, the right of public performance, and the right to display the work. The right to display the work, you may remember, has limited applicability to musical works. But to the copyright owners of visual works such as those listed above this right is extraordinarily important. And the right of public performance is just as vital to the owners of visual works as it is to the owners of musical works.

Since video is the audiovisual medium which educators use most often these days I will, for the remainder of this chapter refer to videos only. But please understand that when I use the word "video" I'm using it as a substitute for all audiovisual media, including films and filmstrips.

Playing a video in a classroom situation is, legally, a public performance which is one of the rights reserved to the copyright owner of the video. So, is it a copyright infringement to show a video in your music classroom? Maybe, maybe not. As with music, there are a number of Fair Uses which apply to the use of videos in school situations. If the use of a video in an educational setting meets all of the following criteria it is a Fair Use and is permitted:

1. The performance must be presented by instructors or pupils; *and*

2. the performance must occur in the course of face-to-face teaching activities; *and*

3. the performance must take place in a classroom or similar place of instruction in a non-profit educational institution; *and*

4. the performance must be of a legally acquired, or legally copied, copy of the work.

Once again, all four criteria must be met. If just one of the four criteria cannot be met, then the performance would, technically, be an infringement.

I think your first test should be to pass the second criteria, the "teaching" requirement. If your showing of the video isn't related to teaching then don't even bother to look at the other three criteria. For example, showing a video as a reward at the end of the year would be an infringement. So would showing one simply for entertainment purposes. It doesn't matter how you acquired the video, legally or otherwise. Showing a video for any purpose other than teaching is an infringement.

I wouldn't recommend stretching the truth on this one, like claiming that showing *Amadeus* to your show choir on the next to last day of school will help them perform better. Be advised that the large companies which own videos and motion pictures actively seek out infringements such as this.

Let's look at some uses which could legitimately be called Fair Uses and then some that aren't. In all cases we'll assume the video was legally acquired. First, legitimate use of videos covered by the Fair Uses:

- A general music teacher shows a video biography of Beethoven during a unit on the lives of great composers.

- During a rehearsal, a band director shows his marching band a video of the finals of a recent drum corps competition.

- During a private lesson, a trumpet teacher shows a video of Wynton Marsalis master class.

- In a conducting class, the instructor shows videos of Leonard Bernstein conducting the New York Philharmonic.

- A soloist is performing a song from the musical *Evita*. You show her the video of the movie version as an example of a performance of the song.

I could go on but I think you get the idea. The use of the video must be related to a teaching situation. It should be closely linked to your lesson plan. Now, video uses which are not Fair Uses:

- A substitute teacher (or the regular teacher, for that matter) plays a video of a Disney movie for a general music class instead of teaching a lesson.

- A choral group performs a medley of songs from *Evita*. On the day after the final spring concert, as a reward or for entertainment, the choral director shows the video of the film version of *Evita*.

- During a band trip, legally acquired videos of recent movies are shown on the VCR system on the bus.

I know, I know...why else would busses have VCR systems if they're not for showing videos? Be advised that this use is technically a copyright infringement. I'm not saying you have to stop doing it, but I am saying that if on the remote chance a film studio found out about it and initiated a lawsuit, you or your school district would probably have some problems.

Basic rule of thumb: if it's for teaching purposes and it's done in school, it passes the test.

A little editorial note here. Film studios, notably those such as Disney and Warner Bros., which create family or children's product or who own cartoon characters, have gotten a lot of criticism in recent years based on their strong defense of their copyrighted and trademarked products. Yes, there have been cases where preschools who painted murals of Disney characters on their walls have been threatened with lawsuits. At times their actions do seem a bit heavy-handed.

And yet, as someone who has spent many years following and researching the subject of copyright, I can't really fault them. Disney makes money from the sale of videos just as music publishers make money from the sale of printed music. That's their product. If you or I bought a Disney video and showed it to dozens of students for entertainment rather than educational purposes, then perhaps the market for the video would shrink by a tiny bit. Multiply that times all the schools in the country and suddenly it's not so small an issue.

As for cartoon characters, they are trademarked properties, a product which can be licensed for significant income. In fact, Warner Bros. Looney Tunes products generate more than $4 billion in sales annually, with significant licensing fees going to Warner Bros. Warner doesn't make the Bugs Bunny T-shirts, they license Bugs' image to the T-shirt manufacturer.

Think of it as similar to Intel, the computer chip manufacturer. As consumers, we don't buy Intel products. We buy products which *contain* an Intel product: a computer chip. And Intel has been so successful at creating an outstanding product and making us aware of it that many computer manufacturers include Intel in their advertising with the "Intel inside" slogan. They know we're more likely to purchase their computer if we know it has "Intel inside." It's the same with Bugs Bunny T-shirts. We buy the T-shirt solely because it has Bugs on it. And Warner Bros. created and developed Bugs, a trademarked character. Trademark law virtually requires that the trademark owner enforce its trademark. If it doesn't, it risks losing the trademark, as the Duncan Company did when it failed to protect its trademark on its most famous product: the yo-yo.

What is a "Legally Acquired Video?"

Let's spend a little time with this because it's somewhat complicated.

There are basically four ways to acquire a video: buy it, rent it, tape it from a television show, or get a dub from someone else.

The first two ways are legal, no question about it. Remember, you still must pass the three other requirements for Fair Use of a video in teaching situations, even with purchased or rented video tapes. But what if the tape you've purchased or rented states "for home use only?" To be blunt, that statement is put there to scare you. In general, any legally acquired tape, including those marked "for home use only" may be used for Fair Use educational purposes assuming the other criteria are met.

The third way of acquiring a video, by taping something off television with your VCR is the complicated one. First of all, in case anyone has any doubts, courts have consistently ruled that it is legal for an individual to tape television shows for the purposes of "time shifting." In other words, if you're going to be out of the house during your favorite TV show, or even if you're not and simply want a copy of the show, taping it to view later is perfectly acceptable. There should be no confusion about this. You are free to make a tape for your own use, watch it as often as you want, alone or with family and friends, or even lend it to friends. The fact that the taped show was broadcast on a network or cable channel makes no difference.

May you use those legal "time shifted" tapes for educational purposes? Here's where things get sticky. First of all, there is a distinction between tapes made of local broadcast channels and cable channels. Local broadcast channels are those channels which you could receive on a TV antenna on your house. In general, that includes affiliates of the major networks and local independent stations. WGN, the Chicago superstation which I receive on my cable system would not be a local broadcast station because I live in South Carolina and could not receive its signal with an antenna. You may make video copies of shows broadcast on local channels for educational use without getting any permission from the broadcaster.

Cable Channels, both regular cable networks such as A&E, The History Channel and so-called "premium" cable channels such as HBO or The Disney Channel are different. There are no Fair Uses specifically for the taping of cable networks. Your use of such tapes in educational situations is governed by the specific cable network's policies toward educational use. Some networks, such as The Discovery Channel or The Weather Channel, are very liberal and may allow you to use a taped video for a specific period of time. Some even publish guides for educators outlining their policies on educational use of their shows. Before using tapes made from shows broadcast on cable networks you should check with the network regarding the use of their shows in educational situations.

Whether you've got a legally made tape of a show from a local broadcaster (for which no prior permission is needed) or from a cable network (which may or may not require checking first with the cable network), there's one huge restriction: the limit on how long you may keep the tape. You may keep it for only 45 days and you may show it to students only during the first 10 school days of that 45 day period.

Why the time limit? *Because the broadcaster is not the copyright owner of the show which you have taped and cannot grant permission for public performance or display.* That permission can only come from the copyright owner of the show. You will need to get permission from the copyright owner of the show if you want to keep the tape beyond the 45 day limit. That time limit is simply an accommodation by copyright law of an educator's immediate use of a taped television show.

Remember all the guidelines in Chapter 6 related to photocopying from books or periodicals for classroom use? Essentially you are permitted to make copies for students for immediate use. Using a copy of the same article or story year after year in the same course is prohibited. The 45 day time limit for videos is basically the same thing. So it would not be permissible to tape a television show in August for use in January unless you obtain permission from the copyright owner of the show. The broadcaster cannot give you this permission.

By the way, what can you do in the remaining days of the 45 day time limit after the first 10 school days? Not much, except review the video yourself.

And finally, what about the fourth way to acquire a video, by getting a dub from someone else? Well, you can pretty much assume that this is not a legally acquired copy.

Incidentally, where a tape is made or who makes it has no bearing on anything I've stated in this chapter. A copy made by a school librarian on school equipment is no different than a copy you made at home.

Making Videos

You may make a single copy of a video of a performance by your group, or a rehearsal, or a lesson, and keep it on file for reference or review. But if you want to make multiple copies and distribute them, either with or without charge, you'll have to get the permission of the copyright owners of each of the musical works contained on the videotape.

It's similar to recording your performing group except that there is no Compulsory Mechanical License which allows you to record a work provided you're prepared to pay a fixed royalty. In other words, you need to get permission from the copyright owner *before* you record. And, there are no established fees for the use of music in videos. In fact, you may be expected to pay two separate fees: a synchronization fee (which fixes the music with the video) and a royalty on each copy distributed. Some publishers may expect no fee, others a modest fee, still others a huge fee. Furthermore, a copyright owner would be within his rights to deny the use of his song in a video.

You can contact the copyright owner directly. However, many publishers use The Harry Fox Agency as a clearing house for video uses of their music, so one letter or phone call to the Fox Agency may be all you need to do. That's especially convenient if there are several musical works on your video. The Fox Agency's address and phone number are listed in the Glossary.

If you hire a professional video company to produce your video find out from them if they plan to obtain clearances for the use of the music and pay any fees that may be required. Someone will have to, and, like recordings, it doesn't matter if you do it or the video company does.

What about videos made by parents of concerts? Well, technically they're an infringement. However, I am not personally aware of any cases where a copyright owner has gotten excited, much less threatened an infringement suit over a parent's video. So I wouldn't worry too much about it, but you should be aware that it is, indeed, an infringement, albeit a benign one.

On the other hand, it sometimes seems that videotaping by parents is getting out of hand, and intrudes upon the enjoyment of the concert by non-videotaping members of the audience. You might try to use "copyright law" as a means of putting a stop to it but you'd probably have a lot of angry parents on your hands. I don't think it's really your responsibility to enforce "copyright law" with respect to parent videotaping. But you might put a simple statement in your concert program: "Videotaping this performance is an infringement of U.S. copyright law." That would seem to get you and your school off the hook in case of any problems; the videotapers have been advised and it's their decision.

If someone such as a parent or a small-time video service gets involved in selling videotapes of a school concert and you or your school is not involved in it, I would definitely urge you to put a stop to it unless the seller goes to all the trouble of getting copyright clearances and paying any fees which may be required by copyright owners. Even then, you get into sticky areas such as the use of your students to generate a profit (if indeed the video service is doing it for profit) without any compensation to the school. From a professional and ethical standpoint it doesn't seem right.

 11 *Computers, Software and the Internet*

When I first began work on this chapter I was afraid it was going to be complicated and difficult. But the more I researched the subject the more I realized that a basic knowledge and understanding of copyright was all I needed. Copyright questions that arise in the computer area are remarkably similar to many of the questions related to other subjects in this book. So if you've read all the previous chapters and have a basic understanding of the principles of copyright you should find this chapter easy to understand.

In 1993, President Clinton established the National Information Infrastructure Task Force. Among other things, the task force was asked to determine how, or if, copyright law needed to be changed to address the internet and computer networks. Surprisingly, in 1994, the task force reported that little needed to be changed in current copyright law to address the internet. Current law, the group seemed to feel, could be applied reasonably well to the online world. And software manufacturers already had plenty of existing copyright statutes dating from a 1980 revision of copyright law which protects them from software pirates and other unauthorized duplicators. So no recommendations were made to Congress to tinker with copyright laws for the computer age.

Software

Back in Chapter 2, *What is Copyright?*, I discussed the fact that copyright is an intangible using an analogy comparing ownership of one share of General Motors stock and ownership of a Chevrolet. Remember? Even if you've paid $20,000 for the Chevrolet you don't own a piece of General Motors, just one of their products. The same is true of music. And it's also true of software.

When you buy software or a computer application either for your computer at home or at school you own the CD-ROM or disk on which the software program is contained. You do not own the software itself. It, of course, is owned by the manufacturer— the copyright owner. And as a copyright owner, the manufacturer enjoys all the same rights as the owner of a piece of music: the right to reproduce, perform, distribute, display, and prepare derivative works. Reproducing, distributing, and displaying are the three most important rights to a software manufacturer.

What rights do you have as the purchaser of the software? They're spelled out on a license agreement usually included either with the software's documentation or as a part of the program itself. These licenses take many different forms. If you're curious, take a look at a few license agreements included with software you already own.

For some you agree to accept the terms of the license by opening the wrapper around the disk or CD-ROM. This is sneaky and, in fact, some states don't even legally recognize such licenses. Most licenses state that you may make a single copy for back-up use.

You can wade through all the legalese if you're really interested in the licenses. Or you can do what I do: I never read any software license agreements, I never make copies to give to friends, and I never accept copies given to me by others. Following that advice will pretty much insure that you won't go astray of copyright laws related to software.

Computer programs are expressly covered by a 1980 revision of U.S. copyright law. Making unauthorized copies of computer software is a felony with fines as high as $250,000 and five years in prison. Of course, those fines are for computer pirates who traffic in huge quantities of unauthorized software, just as record pirates did in the 1950's before music publishers and federal authorities succeeded in shutting them down with huge fines and jail terms. You may not be fined $250,000 if you're caught making copies of software and giving or selling them to others, but if you do it, you're guilty of a felony. Federal authorities, including the FBI, take felonies seriously. And if you're caught you'll face some pretty strong and well financed software industry lawyers.

I don't want to scare you with this; it's always a fine line between advising you of the technical rights and wrongs of copyright and going overboard and causing unnecessary worry. Think of software as being just like printed music. Don't do anything to software that you wouldn't do to printed music and you're safe.

The one big difference between music publishers and software manufacturers is the software manufacturers' aggressiveness in identifying infringers and pursuing them with the full force of law. They've also been successful in getting federal agencies to consider software piracy and infringement as a top priority. So you're playing with fire here if you should decide to go into business as a software pirate.

Some software can be purchased with what's called a "site-license"...that is, you pay a certain amount and you are allowed to make a limited number of copies. This is practical for companies and institutions such as schools. Perhaps your school has purchased a site-license; it's all very common and quite legal. On the other hand, perhaps your school has purchased a single use software program and has installed it on several computers within the school. This is a copyright infringement, pure and simple. And it's an infringement that software manufacturers prosecute. It doesn't matter if the software came on a disk or a CD-ROM. Your school should, as they say in legal terms, cease and desist.

Suppose your school has a network or intranet which allows several computers to share software installed on a server. To use any software with this system legally your school should obtain a network license. Not doing so would technically be an infringement—another one which software manufacturers consider a big no-no. Some software manufacturers permit network use with certain programs, especially for use within one building. Read the license that came with the software.

There's one other way in which software manufacturers differ from music publishers. In 1990 Congress granted them one additional right not granted to music, text, graphics, or any other copyrightable product: the right to control the rental, lease, or lending of software. That's actually pretty amazing. If a similar right had been given to books, there would be no libraries. Congress recognized that and granted a Fair Use for the lending of software by non-profit libraries, provided that a notice is placed on the packaging.

So far I've been discussing commercial software, the kind you can buy in computer stores and from mail-order catalogs. But there are three other kinds of software as well: shareware, freeware, and public domain software. Personally, as a person who makes his living creating music, I've never quite understood any of them. After all, if you're talented enough to create a good product, why should you give it away? Sometimes we, as creative people, undervalue our creative efforts and I've always felt that the programmers of such software were guilty of this. In any event, shareware, freeware, and public domain software are a reality in the computer world and need to be addressed.

Shareware. Shareware is not free. It is, in fact, a marketing technique. The software developer offers his program either online or through some other free distribution system. Users are encouraged to try the program. If they continue to use it, they are expected to pay a fee and register their copy with the shareware owner. Sometimes users receive printed documentation with payment of the fee.

A shareware owner (that is, the person or company which owns the copyright in the program) does not relinquish copyright in the program. It would be as if a music publisher simply sent out thousands of free copies of a vocal solo book and asked anyone who uses it to send a check for the purchase price. It's the honor system taken to extremes.

Using a shareware program beyond the initial trial period prescribed by the shareware owner would be an infringement of copyright. So would re-selling the shareware, or altering it. You should carefully read any "read-me" files which came with shareware to determine exactly what you can and cannot do.

Right now I'm using one piece of software which might be shareware. Or it might be freeware. I can't tell, even after re-reading the "read-me" files. I got it on a floppy disk I received when I renewed a computer magazine subscription. I could send $25 to register my copy, but if I don't, I don't seem to be in violation of the license included in the program. So which is it? Shareware or...

Freeware. Freeware is distributed in much the same way as shareware, except that no payment or registration is required of a user. Sometimes freeware owners ask for a "contribution" but it's not legally required. So I guess that program I'm using is freeware which asks for a contribution.

Like shareware owners, freeware owners do not relinquish copyright in their work. So while you may legally use it for free you may not alter it or sell it.

Public Domain Software. This is software for which the owner has voluntarily relinquished all claim to copyright. You can use it, alter it, sell it, anything. However, any software created since March of 1989 can be dedicated to the public domain only if the owner says so in writing. So do not assume a piece of software is in the public domain unless you see a statement to that effect on the program or packaging.

One more thing about software... Computer documentation (the manuals, user guides, books and videos which may accompany a software program) is covered by copyright which is unrelated to the copyright in the software itself. Treat these materials just as you would any other book or video. Making copies without permission, even of charts or visual guides, would technically be a copyright infringement.

The Internet

It's been said that copyright should not, or perhaps does not, exist on the internet. Or if it exists, it is impossible to police. There's some truth to the second statement. Policing copyright infringements on the net is sometimes extraordinarily difficult. Infringements such as sending copyrighted files or software from one computer to another can be virtually untraceable. So, is copyright impossible to maintain on the net?

No, because certain activities *can* be traced, sometimes very easily, and because associations of copyright owners such as the Software Publishers Association regularly scan online services such as America Online, CompuServe, and bulletin board services for infringements. So do large corporations that derive income from their copyrighted properties. Music organizations also scan the world wide web for infringements. All are looking to find cases they can't lose in order to make an example of the infringer.

In fact, there now exist internet "spiders" similar to search vehicles which can be programmed to search for words or phrases which would indicate a copyright infringement. For example, a music publisher could search for a line of text in one of its songs and locate every instance of it on the internet. But I'm getting a little ahead of myself.

There's a general feeling that anything posted online is free or dedicated to the public for its free use. Indeed, it is "free" in the economic sense just as broadcast television is "free."

Consider the delicate balance copyright law must hold between creators and users. Creators have rights (including the five basic rights to reproduce, perform, distribute, display, and prepare derivative works) and users have certain limited free and fair uses of the creators' works. That balance is not obviated because a creative work is placed online. There are plenty of unjustified justifications for unlimited use of online material, just as there are for illegally photocopying music. But few of those justifications are legal.

To better understand copyrights online it might be easier to think of the internet as television. That's what an instructor told me at an internet seminar I once attended. He said, "Folks, the internet is television!" I've been thinking of it that way ever since and that concept has made it easier for me to understand copyrights on the internet.

As described in Chapter 10, courts have allowed videotaping of television for personal use under certain circumstances. If you want to do something else besides watch it with family and friends you start running into problems. So it is with the internet. View it as often as you wish, download legally posted files, games, and programs which are offered to you, keep them on your computer for your own use, and you shouldn't have any problems.

Begin by assuming that any website you view is protected by copyright. This is true even if there's no copyright notice shown. Under international copyright conventions no notice is required. Some sites make it plain that they are "free" to the public and no copyright is claimed (like public domain software). But unless you see such a statement the website is protected by copyright, even if the creator of the site makes no effort to claim copyright.

Be advised that there are no Fair Uses devoted exclusively to the internet, at least not yet. But applying guidelines for Fair Uses of printed materials would seem to be prudent. The most applicable guidelines are:

- The purpose and character of the use.

- The amount of material copied.

- The effect of the use on the market for the work.

So displaying a website to a classroom would appear to be OK but copying the contents of a website to a school computer for reference or use at a later date might not be. Please note: I'm in uncharted waters here. As I said, there are no guidelines for Fair Uses specific to the internet and international conventions regarding copyright have yet to be developed fully. So I'm a little reluctant to give you specific do's and don'ts. Use what you've learned about copyright, apply the print guidelines listed above, and do what you think is best.

In other areas I can be a little more specific.

For example, computer code (the actual programming) is protected by copyright. It's common practice for amateur website creators to download websites they find attractive and use the computer code for the site as the basis for a new site, cutting and pasting where necessary. This infringes on the copyright owner's right to create a derivative work and is clearly a copyright infringement. It's something your students may be fooling around with so be advised.

What about music online? Thousands of copyrighted musical works have been placed online without authorization of the owners of the songs. They're available to be downloaded. Both the person who placed the song on line and the person who downloaded it are infringers. Music publishers are aggressively pursuing these infringers. The first and most important case involving music on the internet was Frank Music vs. CompuServe.

As a result of Frank Music vs. CompuServe, music publishers have established that downloading of music files on the internet is a mechanical use. Online services such as America Online and CompuServe are now responsible for musical works posted on their service and for the payment of mechanical royalties for each downloading of a musical work. Music that's uploaded from AOL or CompuServe members should be intercepted by the on line service and the uploader will be required to identify himself. Much of this online use of music is licensed by

The Harry Fox Agency, the same agency that represents many publishers in the matter of recordings. So licensing of music on the internet is becoming a reality, slowly, according to the Fox Agency, but surely.

It also appears that software publishers are stepping up their surveillance of bulletin board services. So are other individual copyright owners. Flagrant copyright infringements will not be tolerated in the future, I predict. Each year will bring more court cases resulting in victories for copyright owners. In spite of the desire of many for the internet to be free of copyright restrictions, courts and Congress simply will not allow this to happen. Perhaps individual infringements cannot be stopped given the nature of the internet and its international scope. But specific laws will be passed and court precedents will be set.

Even with the international scope of the internet strides have been made. In 1996, negotiators from 160 countries reached an agreement on new, global copyright agreements which address the internet and computer data. Among other things, the agreement specifically extends copyright protection of music to the internet and computer generated copies of recordings, and that online copyright owners would be granted the right to regulate the distribution of copyrighted materials. To balance those rights with the rights of users, temporary downloaded copies would not be considered an infringement. The agreement must be ratified by each country, but it clearly indicates which way copyright laws are headed with respect to the internet.

Regarding software and graphics, precedents have already been set with important court cases in the U.S. In one, the computer game company Sega won a case against a bulletin board service which blatantly and openly made new Sega games available to be downloaded. I suspect a similar case will be made someday against services who offer unauthorized digital files of songs.

As for graphics, in a highly publicized case, *Playboy* magazine won an out-of-court settlement of $500,000 from a bulletin board service which openly posted photographs from *Playboy* for downloading. The bulletin board service protested that it didn't do the posting, its members did. But the court ruled that the evidence was overwhelming that the bulletin board service was aware that many of the files posted by its members were from *Playboy*...so overwhelming, in fact, that the judge ruled in favor of *Playboy* on what's called a summary judgment prior to the trial. That is, the evidence was so great that there was nothing the defendant could possibly put forth in a trial to claim innocence. This precedent, too, could be applied to music.

Which brings me to another item related to computers: the scanner. Just as I suggested you think of the internet as television, I'm suggesting you think of your scanner as a photocopy machine. Don't scan anything you wouldn't photocopy and you'll be OK. Scan a copyrighted article and save it on your computer for reference. That's OK. But don't print it out six months later, photocopy it, and distribute copies to your music appreciation class. That would violate the Fair Uses for educational use of copied materials.

Finally, a word about music notation programs such as Finale. Yes, these programs make it easy to create professional-looking music for your students. It's simple to write a melody line and text of a pop song, make copies and distribute them to your students. But just because it's easy doesn't make it right. You're making a copy of a copyrighted musical work...not a photocopy but a copy nonetheless...and it's a copyright infringement.

PART IV
Recapitulation

12 *Useful Information*

The Difference Between a Copyright Owner and a Publisher

A century ago, when the only way to distribute a song was to print it, music publishers almost always owned the copyright in a work they published. Today, however, a publisher who prints an edition of a musical work is not necessarily the copyright owner of that work. In other words, not all music publishers actually print their own music. In the field of popular music especially, very few pop music publishers print and sell their own songs anymore. Indeed, most rely on the services of a "print publisher"—a music publisher who specializes in printed music.

One of the exclusive rights granted to copyright owners is the right to make copies. Copyright owners of pop songs sell or "license" their right to make copies (known as the "print right") to other publishers who specialize in printing music. In fact, the copyright owner may further divide his print right, and license several print publishers to sell various editions or arrangements.

For example, Hal Leonard prints and sells the songs from the Disney movie *Hercules*, but the copyrights in the songs are owned by Disney.

The copyright owner of a piece of music is always identified in the copyright notice shown at the bottom of the first page of music on a printed edition. If you don't know the copyright owner's address, the print publisher who issued the edition can give it to you.

How to Read a Copyright Notice

A copyright notice can tell you a great deal about a piece of published music. At the very least it tells you how old the work is and who controls the copyright. In its simplest form, a copyright notice looks like this:

Copyright 1998, Jay Althouse

A simple notice such as the one above satisfies the requirements of the Copyright Office. It contains the word "copyright," indicating the work is protected by copyright, the year in which copyright is claimed, and the name of the copyright owner.

Many publishers use more complex notices which provide more information. For example:

© 1998, Right Hand Music, Nashville, TN
International Copyright Secured. All Rights Reserved.

The symbol © is the international symbol for the word "copyright" and is recognized by any nation which is a signatory to international copyright conventions. Publishers use © in order to secure international copyright protection in such nations, provided they have complied with other international copyright formalities. In this case the copyright owner, Right Hand Music, has listed the city in which it is located. "International Copyright Secured" means that the publisher has complied with international copyright formalities and claims copyright around the world, but it's redundant, since © accomplishes the same thing. "All Rights Reserved" means that Right Hand Music retains all rights in the work.

Here's an even more complex notice:

© Copyright MCMXCVIII, Right Hand Music (ASCAP), Nashville, TN
All Rights Administered by Queen Street Music,
130 Queen Street, Brentwood, TN 37027
This Arrangement © MCMXCVIII, Right Hand Music
International Copyright Secured. All Rights Reserved.
SOLE SELLING AGENT FOR THIS ARRANGEMENT: ALFRED PUBLISHING CO.

Line 1: Here © and the word "copyright" are both used. It's redundant but doesn't hurt. Some publishers like Roman numerals. (Why? Because it's harder to figure out the date that way, but when we hit 2000, it'll be pretty simple: MM.) This piece was originally registered with the Copyright Office in 1998 by Right Hand Music, an ASCAP publisher member located in Nashville.

Line 2: A second publisher, Queen Street Music, located in Brentwood, TN, administers all rights in the song. Right Hand Music probably doesn't have the resources to promote the song so it has engaged Queen Street Music to do so. Queen Street Music lists its complete address, which is very helpful. I've often wondered why more copyright owners don't do this.

Line 3: Arrangements are copyrightable, and this line indicates that a copyright is claimed on the arrangement in addition to the copyright claimed on the basic work. The year date of copyright on the arrangement is 1998 and Right Hand Music is also the owner of the arrangement.

Line 4: Same as the previous example.

Line 5: Queen Street Music, which administers all rights in the song, has granted a license to Alfred Publishing Co. to print the arrangement. Note, however, that Alfred is not the copyright owner of the song or even of the arrangement. It is simply the "sole selling agent" for this particular arrangement of the song.

Who would you contact if you wanted to record the song with this copyright notice? Queen Street Music, the company that administers all rights in the work.

In some cases there may be more than one copyright owner of a musical work. This is usually true in the case of recent pop songs with more than one writer. The copyright notice would then look like this:

> © 1998, Right Hand Music and Queen Street Music
> International Copyright Secured. All Rights Reserved.

Contact either copyright owner if you want to use a work having more than one owner. Sometimes one of the two owners administers the song, and often that information is provided in the copyright notice. But if you contact the one that doesn't, they will usually refer you to the one that does.

In the case of older works a copyright notice may indicate that the copyright has been renewed after its first 28-year term of copyright, like this:

> © Copyright 1951, Swinging Music Company
> U.S. Copyright Renewed
> International Copyright Secured. All Rights Reserved.

A notice stating that the copyright has been renewed is not required by law. And for some categories of works new laws have made renewal automatic. So you should always assume that popular or well-known works published prior to 1978 have been renewed.

Remember, copyrights can change hands. If you have a published edition of a work showing a copyright notice with a previous owner it is not incorrect—just out of date. Newer editions will show the new owner. And also remember that if you can't track down the owner, that doesn't mean you're free to use the piece as you wish.

Copyright notices are not required to be shown for recordings. I never could understand why, but they're not. Most recording companies list writer credits and the performing rights organization (usually ASCAP or BMI) which controls performing rights in the work. Some also identify the publisher.

Performances contained on recordings are copyrightable. As an example, Frank Sinatra's recording of Cole Porter's song, *I've Got You Under My Skin* is a copyrighted entity separate from the copyright in the song itself. Recording companies protect themselves from recording pirates with the copyrights they claim in the recorded performances. The symbol ℗ signifies that copyright is claimed on the performances contained on the recording. Like ©, ℗ is recognized internationally.

Duration of Copyright

Works registered with the Copyright Office on or after January 1, 1978. For works by one writer, copyright subsists until 50 years after the death of the writer. If there is more than one writer, the copyright subsists until 50 years after the death of the last surviving writer. In the case of anonymous or pseudonymous works, the term is 75 years from the date of publication or 100 years from the date of creation, whichever is first.

Works registered with the Copyright Office before January 1, 1978. The Copyright Act of 1976 took effect January 1, 1978 so works registered before that date were covered by the Act of 1909. The Act of 1909 provided for a copyright term of 28 years with a 28 year renewal term. Works registered under the 1909 Act had to be renewed after the first 28 year term. However, the 1976 Act extended the second 28 year term to 47 years for a total of 75 years.

In both of the above cases the copyright subsists until the end of the calendar year. In other words, if the author of a work written in 1980 died on February 1, 1990 the copyright will subsist until December 31, 2040, 50 years from February 1, 1990 plus the end of the calendar year. A work published on February 1, 1930 will remain protected by copyright until December 31, 2005. These works will fall into the Public Domain on January 1, 2040 and January 1, 2006, respectively.

It's pretty safe to say that once a work falls into the Public Domain the copyright cannot be reclaimed or "brought back to life."

There have been some exceptions in recent years, mostly involving works from former European Communist countries such as the Soviet Union. These countries were not signatories to international copyright conventions and did not recognize the copyrights of other Western nations. Accordingly, we didn't recognize their works. But since the fall of Communism in Europe recent copyright accords brought this "if you don't recognize our works, we won't recognize yours" spat to an end. The result is that many twentieth century works by Russian composers which were previously considered to be in the Public Domain in the United States are now once again protected by copyright. So if you plan on doing any band transcriptions of twentieth century Russian orchestral music, I'd suggest you check the the copyright status of the work very carefully before starting.

And finally, remember that arrangements are copyrightable. Thus a published arrangement of a work in the Public Domain is protected by copyright. If, for example, you wish to make a handbell arrangement of a simplified, published piano edition of a Mozart work, you'll have to check with the owner of the piano edition even though the basic work by Mozart is obviously in the Public Domain.

Penalties for Infringers

If a copyright owner successfully sues a copyright infringer, the copyright owner may elect to recover actual damages or statutory damages—specific penalties outlined in the Act of 1976. Actual damages are those suffered by the copyright owner as a result of the infringement and any profits that are attributed to the infringement. For statutory damages a court must award at least $250 but no more than $10,000 for each work infringed upon. In other words, if you were found guilty in court of infringement for photocopying six choral works your liability could theoretically be as much as $60,000. The law also provides for "exceptional cases" in which the maximum penalty could be raised to $50,000 per work infringed or the minimum penalty reduced to $100.

In addition, the Act of 1976 defines four specific types of infringements as criminal offenses.

- Criminal infringement—willful infringement for purposes of commercial or financial gain;

- Fraudulent use of copyright notice—to knowingly place a fraudulent notice on an article or to knowingly distribute a work containing such notice;

- Fraudulent removal of a copyright notice;

- False representation—to knowingly make a false representation in an application for copyright registration.

In the case of willful infringement for commercial gain, the penalty is not more than $10,000 and/or imprisonment for not more than one year for each work infringed (marching band and show/jazz choir arrangers take note). The other three willful infringements have a maximum fine of $2,500.

How to Register a Claim for Copyright

If you've written a musical work or an arrangement of a work in the Public Domain, what must you do to secure copyright protection? Technically, nothing. Under the Act of 1976, a work is protected by copyright automatically when the work is first fixed in a copy or a recording.

However, in order to take advantage of the full benefits of statutory copyright protection, the work should be registered with the Copyright Office, Library of Congress, Washington, DC 20559.

First, you need a proper registration form. Different types of works require different applications. A textbook requires a different application from a song, for example. Write the Copyright Office for the appropriate form. In the case of a musical work you'll need an application for a work of the performing arts. You can request applications and forms by mail or from their website, which is listed in the Glossary.

Complete the application and follow the instructions provided by the Copyright Office, providing a copy of the work, or occasionally two copies, as required by the application.

Note that your application is merely a claim for copyright protection. It's not like a patent application which is researched by the Patent Office and approved only if no similar patent has been granted. The Copyright Office does not research applications. In fact, it registers every application made, legitimate or not, provided the application is completed correctly and all the requirements of registration are fulfilled. If your work infringes on a work for which a previous claim of copyright was made, it's up to the owner of that work to protect his claim, usually with a lawsuit against you. Conversely, it's your responsibility to do the same if someone infringes on your registered work. The Copyright Office won't do it for you.

One last note: titles of works are not copyrightable. Copyright protects a work identified by a certain title, even if another work has the same title.

Sample Letters

On the following pages are sample letters requesting a mechanical license, permission to reprint an out-of-print work, and permission to make an arrangement.

FOR A RECORDING

Anytown High School
1029 School Street
Anytown, PA 18204

February 1, 1998

Alfred Publishing Co., Inc.
P.O. Box 10003
Van Nuys, CA 91410

Dear Sirs:

Please send a mechanical license for *Port Royal Overture* by John O'Reilly to Anytown High School Music Department at the above address.

We are selling a CD of our Spring concert in order to raise money for new instruments. We will be manufacturing approximately 500 copies of the CD.

Sincerely,

John Duncan
Band Director

Instead of writing to each individual publisher, you may also request a mechanical license from the Harry Fox Agency, which represents many publishers in the matter of recordings.

> Anytown High School
> 1029 School Street
> Anytown, PA 18204

February 1, 1998

The Harry Fox Agency, Inc.
711 Third Avenue
New York, NY 10017

Dear Sirs:

Please send a mechanical license to Anytown High School Music Department at the above address for the following works:

TITLE	WRITER	PUBLISHER
One Star	Sally Albrecht /Jay Althouse	Alfred Publishing Co.
Arise My Love, My Fair One	Sherri Porterfield	Alfred Publishing Co.
All Around the World Tonight	Jerry Estes	Heritage Music Press
Sing to the Holy Child	Patrick Liebergen	Harold Flammer Music

We will be producing approximately 500 copies of a CD containing these works.

Sincerely,

Cathy Duncan
Choral Director

FOR A WORK THAT IS OUT OF PRINT

Anytown High School
1029 School Street
Anytown, PA 18204

February 1, 1998
Alfred Publishing Co., Inc.
P.O. Box 10003
Van Nuys, CA 91410

Dear Sirs:

I understand that *For a Time* by John Anderson, which was published by you, is no longer in print.

I have 20 copies which I purchased a few years ago and now need an additional 15 copies because my choir has grown in size.

May I have your permission to make 15 photocopies of *For a Time* for use by my choral group?

Sincerely,

Cathy Duncan
Choral Director

FOR AN ARRANGEMENT

Anytown High School
1029 School Street
Anytown, PA 18204

February 1, 1998

Alfred Publishing Co., Inc.
P.O. Box 10003
Van Nuys, CA 91410

Dear Sirs:

I would like to make an arrangement for my school marching band of *Port Royal Overture* by John O'Reilly, which is published in concert band version by your company.

If permission is granted I will prepare a score and parts for the 96 band members. The arrangement will be performed solely by the Anytown High School Big Red Marching Band during the 1998 season.

Sincerely,

John Duncan
Band Director

13 *Glossary*

The number in parenthesis refers to the chapter containing more information.

ASCAP - See **American Society of Composers, Authors and Publishers**

American Society of Composers, Authors and Publishers - The first **performing rights organization** in the United States, founded in 1914. One Lincoln Plaza, New York, NY 10023. 212-621-6000. Website: www.ascap.com. (8)

BMI - See Broadcast Music, Inc.

Blanket Performing License - A **license** purchased from a **performing rights organization**. The licensee obtains the **performance right** for all works written and/or published by all the organization's members. (8)

Broadcast Music, Inc. - A U.S. **performing rights organization**, founded in 1939. 320 West 57th Street, New York, NY 10019. 212-586-2000. Website: www.bmi.com. (8)

Compulsory Mechanical License - A limitation on the **mechanical right** by which anyone may record a musical work provided he complies with certain formalities including the payment of the **statutory mechanical royalty**. Also called the **statutory mechanical license**. (3, 7)

Copyright Act of 1790 - The first United States copyright act. Granted copyright protection to books, maps, and charts. (3)

Copyright Act of 1831 - The first United States copyright act to grant copyright protection to musical works. (3)

Copyright Act of 1909 - A general revision of copyright law in the United States. The first law to recognize the **mechanical right**. It also strengthened the **performance right**. Remained in effect until January 1, 1978. (3, 7)

Copyright Act of 1976 - The copyright act presently in effect in the United States. Became law January 1, 1978. (3, 4, 5, 6, 7, 8, 9, 10, 11, 12)

Copyright Infringement - A violation of any of the exclusive rights granted by law to a **copyright owner**. (4, 5, 6, 7, 8, 9, 10, 11, 12)

Copyright Owner - The owner(s) of any or all of the exclusive rights granted under copyright law. One particular work can have more than one copyright owner. (3)

Derivative Work - A work based on one or more preexisting works, such as an arrangement, dramatization, transcription, orchestration or simplified edition. (9)

Dramatic Work - A work of the performing arts, such as a play, musical play, opera, or ballet, which is primarily dramatic in nature. (8)

Exempt Performance - A **public performance** covered by one or more of the limitations placed upon the **performance right** by the **Copyright Act of 1976**. (8)

Fair Use - A limitation placed on an exclusive right of a **copyright owner**. (5, 6, 7, 8, 10, 11)

Grand Rights - Another name for **performance rights** in **dramatic works**. (8)

Harry Fox Agency, Inc., The - An agent used by many **copyright owners** for the licensing of recordings of their musical works. 711 3rd Avenue, New York, NY 10017. 212-370-5330. Website: www.nmpa.org/hfa.html (7, 10, 12)

Infringement - See **copyright infringement**.

License - A grant of one or more of the exclusive rights of **copyright owners** by the owner of that right to another party. (7, 9)

Literary Work - A **non-dramatic work** of prose or poetry. (6)

Mechanical Right - One of the exclusive rights granted to **copyright owners**: the right to record the copyrighted work. So-called because the first recording devices were known as "mechanical instruments." (3, 7, 12)

Music Publishers Association of the U.S. - An association of publishers or primarily serious and/or educational music. 1562 First Ave., Suite 246, New York, NY 10028. Website: www.mpa.org(5)

Musical Play - A **dramatic work**, such as a musical, musical comedy, or operetta, incorporating music as an integral part of the work. (8)

National Music Publishers Association - An association of publishers of primarily popular music. 711 3rd Avenue, 8th Floor, New York, NY 10017. 212-370-5330. Website: www.nmpa.org (5)

Non-dramatic Work - A work of the performing arts, such as a musical work, which is not dramatic in nature (8).

Non-exempt Performance - A **public performance** which falls under the purview of the **performance right**. (8)

Out-of-print Music - A music publication which is no longer available for sale. A copyright on a musical work does not expire when the work is placed out of print. (5)

Parody Lyrics - Any lyric which replaces the original lyric of a vocal work. (9)

Performance Right - One of the exclusive rights granted to **copyright owners**: the right to publicly perform the work. (4, 8, 10)

Performing Rights Organization - An organization which administers the **performance rights** in musical works for its **publisher** and writer members. In the United States, **ASCAP, BMI,** and **SESAC.** (8)

Print Right - One of the exclusive rights granted to **copyright owners**: the right to print copies of the work. (4, 5, 6)

Public Domain - The absence of copyright. A work is in the Public Domain if no copyright is claimed on the work or if the copyright in the work has expired. Arrangements of works in the Public Domain are copyrightable, however. (12)

Public Performance - To perform or display a work at a public place live or by any device or process capable of transmitting or recording an image of a performance or display. (8, 10)

Published Work - A work which has been distributed to the public in copies or recordings by sale, rental, lease, or lending. (5, 6)

Publisher - One who issues a printed edition of a work. May or may not be the **copyright owner** of the work. (12)

Recording Right - see **mechanical right**.

Register of Copyrights - The director of the **United States Copyright Office**. (4)

Rental Music - Music which is distributed through the rental of scores and/or parts rather than through the sale of copies. Under present copyright law, a rental work is considered a **published work**, and afforded the same copyright protection.

SESAC - The smallest of the three **performing rights organizations** in the U.S. (8)

Small Rights - Another name for **performance rights** in **nondramatic works**. (8)

Software Publishers Association - An association of publishers and manufacturers of computer software. 1730 M Street, N.W., Washington, DC 20036. 202-452-1600 or 800-388-7478. Website: www.spa.org (11)

Statute of Anne - A 1709 British law recognized as the first true copyright law anywhere in the world. (3)

Statutory Mechanical License - see **compulsory mechanical license**

Statutory Mechanical Royalty - The royalty required under the terms of the compulsory mechanical license. (7)

Synchronization Right - The right to affix, or synchronize, a musical work in an audio-visual work such as a film or video. (10)

Universal Copyright Convention - An organization of nations, all of which agree to provide copyright protection in their countries to copyright works from all member nations. The United States is a member.

United States Copyright Office - The division of the Library of Congress which registers copyrights in the United States. Library of Congress, Washington, DC 20559. 202-479-0700 (202-707-9100 to order forms and circulars). Website: lcweb.loc.gov/copyright/ (3, 4, 12)

Unpublished Work - A work which has not been distributed to the public in copies or recordings by sale, rental, lease, or lending. Unpublished works may be protected by copyright.

Informative Copyright Websites

ASCAP (http://www.ascap.com) - Includes a searchable database of all ASCAP titles, information on copyright, and information about ASCAP and performing rights.

Association of American Publishers (http://www.publishers.org) - Valuable copyright information relating to books and text from an association of book publishers.

BMI (http://www.bmi.com) - Similar to ASCAP's site, including a searchable database of all BMI titles.

Copyright Clearance Center (http://www.copyright.com) - Offers information on obtaining a license to make photocopies of text (not music) materials.

Copyright Website (http://www.benedict.com) - A jam-packed site relating to copyright in all forms, including music. A good general information site, it's informative, easy-to-understand, and filled with interesting facts. Check here if you want information on copyright subjects other than music.

The Harry Fox Agency (http://www.nmpa.org/hfa.html) - Before you make a recording check out this site. Includes all the information you will need related to royalties in recordings including the current statutory mechanical rate. Includes searchable databases of songs and publishers, useful for tracking down copyright owners for recordings or videos.

Music Library Association Guide to Copyright for Music Librarians (http://www.musiclibraryassoc.org/Copyright/ copyhome.htm) - Good general information site. Its best feature is a list of Frequently Asked Questions which may be helpful in answering questions not specifically addressed in this book.

Music Publishers Association of the U.S. (http://www.mpa.org) - Very helpful to music educators. Includes many links and an easy way to request brochures for more information on copyright relating to music.

National Music Publishers Association (http://www.nmpa.org) - Parent of Harry Fox Organization. Interesting copyright information and helpful advice.

Stanford University Libraries Comprehensive Copyright Site (http://fairuse.stanford.edu/) - An outstanding and comprehensive site including information on copyright history, statutes, judicial opinions, regulations, treaties, and articles on dozens of copyright subjects. The best features are the dozens of links to other copyright-related sites. An excellent resource both for music and non-musical copyright subjects.

United States Copyright Office (http://www.lcweb.loc.gov/copyright/) - Up-to-date and complete information on U.S. copyright law. This is the site to visit to get information on pending legislation and changes in copyright law.

About The Author

Jay Althouse received a B.S. degree in Music Education and an M.Ed. degree in Music from Indiana University of Pennsylvania. For eight years he served as a rights and licenses administrator for a major educational music publisher. During that time he served a term on the Executive Board of the Music Publishers Association of America.

As a composer of choral music, Mr. Althouse has over 400 works in print for choirs of all levels. His music is widely performed throughout the English-speaking world. He is a writer member of ASCAP and is a regular recipient of the ASCAP Special Award for his compositions in the area of standard music.

His book, *Copyright: The Complete Guide for Music Educators* has been in print continuously since 1984 and is recognized as the definitive sourcebook on the subject of copyright for music educators. Mr. Althouse has also co-written several musicals for children with his wife, Sally K. Albrecht, compiled and arranged a number of highly regarded vocal solo collections, and is the co-writer, with Russell Robinson, of the best-selling book *The Complete Choral Warm-up Book*, published by Alfred Publishing Co., Inc.